Lead, kindly Light

John henry Cardinal Newman

A Devotional Sa
Compiled and Edi
Hal M. Helm

PARACLETE
PRESS

Third Printing, April 1995

©1987 by Paraclete Press
Library of Congress #: 87-60611
ISBN: 0-941478-78-5
All rights reserved.
Published by Paraclete Press
Orleans, Massachusetts
Printed in the United States of America

CONTENTS

LEAD, KINDLY LIGHT

Lead, kindly Light, amid the encircling gloom,
  Lead thou me on;
The night is dark, and I am far from home;
  Lead thou me on:
Keep thou my feet; I do not ask to see
The distant scene; one step enough for me.

I was not ever thus, nor prayed that thou
  Shouldst lead me on;
I loved to choose and see my path; but now
  Lead thou me on.
I loved the garish day, and, spite of fears,
Pride ruled my will: remember not past years.

So long thy power hath blest me, sure it still
  Will lead me on
O'er moor and fen, o'er crag and torrent, till
  The night is gone;
And with the morn those angel faces smile
Which I have loved long since, and lost awhile.

INTRODUCTION

This collection of writings of John Henry Cardinal Newman is a personal selection. Included are most of his posthumous *Meditations and Devotions*, abridged forms of some of his *Plain and Parochial Sermons*, and several of his poems. I have added an essay on his long and fruitful life at the end of the book. It is hoped that the present selection will serve as an introduction to Newman to some who might never pick up one of the eight volumes of *Plain and Parochial Sermons* or read one of the scores of books on his contribution to theological, philosophical and educational thought.

When he was raised to the cardinalate, Fr. Newman chose as his motto the words *Cor ad cor loquitur,* "heart speaks to heart." The Newman presented here is one who speaks "heart to heart." He calls us to a life of faith, holiness and love. He exposes some of the hidden barriers we meet on our spiritual pilgrimage, and some of the easy bypaths which we might be tempted to take.

People have asked, "Why are you bringing out a book of Newman writings?" My answer has been, "I'm not quite sure." I felt drawn to him — possibly because I love and have been moved by his great hymns, or it may be that Another drew me to explore some of the riches we have been bequeathed from his long and fruitful life. At any rate, it has been a fascinating and rewarding undertaking.

Hal M. Helms

HOPE IN GOD
—CREATOR

FIRST MEDITATION

God has created all things for good; all things for their greatest good; everything for its own good. What is the good of one is not the good of another; what makes one man happy would make another unhappy. God has determined, unless I interfere with His plan, that I should reach that which will be my greatest happiness. He looks on me individually, He calls me by my name, He knows what I can do, what I can best be, what is my greatest happiness, and He means to give it to me.

God knows what is my greatest happiness, but I do not. There is no rule about what is happy and good; what suits one would not suit another. And the ways by which perfection is reached vary very much. The medicines necessary for our souls are very different from each other. Thus God leads us by strange ways. We know He wills our happiness, but we neither know what our happiness is nor the way. We are blind. Left to ourselves we would take the wrong way. We must leave it to Him.

Let us put ourselves into His hands, and not be startled though He leads us by a strange way, a

5

mirabilis via, as the Church speaks. Let us be sure He will lead us aright, that He will bring us to that which is, not indeed what *we* think best, not what is best for another, but what is best for us.

PRAYER

O my God, I will put myself without reserve into Thy hands. Wealth or woe, joy or sorrow, friends or bereavement, honor or humiliation, good report or ill report, comfort or discomfort, Thy presence or the hiding of Thy countenance, all is good if it comes from Thee. Thou art wisdom and Thou art love — what can I desire more? Thou hast led me in Thy counsel, and with glory hast Thou received me. What have I in heaven, and apart from Thee what do I desire upon earth? My flesh and my heart faileth; but God is the God of my heart, and my portion for ever.

SECOND MEDITATION

God was all-complete, all-blessed in Himself; but it was His will to create a world for His glory. He is Almighty, and might have done all things Himself, but it has been His will to bring about His purposes by the beings He has created. We are all created to His glory — we are created to do His will. I am created to do something or to be something for which no one else is created; I have a place in God's counsels, in God's world, which no one else has. Whether I be rich or poor, despised or esteemed by man, God knows me and calls me by my name.

God has created me to do some definite service. He has committed some work to me which He has not committed to another. I have my mission — I may never know it in this life, but I shall be told it in the next. Somehow I am necessary for His purposes, as necessary in my place as an Archangel in his. If, indeed, I fail, He can raise another, as He could make the stones children of Abraham. Yet I have a part in this great work. I am a link in a chain, a bond of connection between persons. He has not created me for nothing. I shall do good, I shall do His work. I shall be an angel of peace, a preacher of truth in my own place, while not intending it, if I do but keep His commandments and serve Him in my calling.

Therefore I will trust Him. Whatever, wherever I am, I can never be thrown away. If I am in sickness, my sickness may serve Him; in perplexity, my perplexity may serve Him. If I am in sorrow, my sorrow may serve Him. My sickness, or perplexity, or sorrow may be necessary causes of some great end, which is quite beyond us. He does nothing in vain. He may prolong my life, He may shorten it. He knows what He is about. He may take away my friends, He may throw me among strangers, He may make me feel desolate, make my spirits sink, hide the future from me — still He knows what He is about.

PRAYER

O Adonai, O Ruler of Israel, Thou who guidest Joseph like a flock, O Emmanuel, O Sapientia, O Wisdom, I give myself to Thee. I trust Thee wholly. Thou art wiser than I — more loving to me than I myself. Deign to fulfill Thy high purposes in me whatever they be — work in and through me. I am

born to serve Thee, to be Thine, to be Thy instrument.
Let me be Thy blind instrument. I ask not to see — I
ask not to know — I ask simply to be used.

THIRD MEDITATION

*What mind of man can imagine the love which the
Eternal Father bears towards the Only Begotten Son?* It
has been from everlasting — and it is infinite. So great
is it that divines call the Holy Spirit by the name of that
love, as if to express its infinitude and perfection. Yet
reflect, O my soul, and bow down before the awesome
mystery, that, as the Father loves the Son, so doth the
Son love thee, if thou art one of His elect. For He says
expressly, "As the Father hath loved Me, I also have
loved you. Abide in My love." What mystery in the
whole circle of revealed truths is greater than this?

*The love which the Son bears to thee, a creature, is
like that which the Father bears to the uncreated Son.*
O wonderful mystery! *This*, then, is the history of what
else is so strange: that He should have taken my flesh
and died for me. The former mystery anticipates the
latter; the latter does but fulfill the former. If He did
not love me so inexpressibly, He would not have suffered for me. I understand now why He died for me,
because He loved me as a father loves his son — not as a
human father merely, but as the Eternal Father loves
the Eternal Son. I see now the meaning of that otherwise inexplicable humiliation: He preferred to regain
me rather than to create new worlds.

How constant He is in His affection! He has loved us
from the time of Adam. He has said from the beginning,

"I will never leave thee nor forsake thee." He did not forsake us in our sin. He did not forsake me. He found me out and regained me. He made a point of it — He resolved to restore me, in spite of myself, to that blessed place which I was so obstinately set against. And now what does He ask of me, but that, as He has loved me with an everlasting love, so I should love Him in such poor measure as I can show.

PRAYER

O mystery of mysteries, that the ineffable love of the Father to the Son should be the love of the Son to us! Why was it, O Lord? What good thing didst Thou see in me a sinner? Why wast Thou set on me? "What is man, that Thou art mindful of him, and the son of man that Thou visitest him?" This poor flesh of mine, this weak sinful soul, which has not life except in Thy grace, Thou didst set Thy love upon it. Complete Thy work, O Lord, and as Thou hast loved me from the beginning, so make me love Thee unto the end.

HOPE IN GOD
—REDEEMER

THE MENTAL SUFFERINGS OF OUR LORD

After all His discourses were fully finished and brought to an end, our Lord said, "The Son of Man will be delivered up to be crucified." (Matt. 26:2) As an army puts itself in battle array, as sailors, before an action, clear the decks, as dying men make their will and then turn to God, so though our Lord could never cease to speak good words, did He sum up and complete His teaching, and then commence His passion. Then He removed by His own act the prohibition which kept Satan from Him, and opened the door to the agitations of His human heart, as a soldier, who is to suffer death, may drop his handkerchief himself. At once Satan came on and seized upon his brief hour.

An evil temper of murmuring and criticism is spread among the disciples. One was the source of it, but it seems to have been spread. The thought of His death was before Him, and He was thinking of it and His burial after it. A woman came and anointed His sacred head. The action spread a soothing tender feeling over His pure soul. It was a mute token of sympathy, and the whole house was filled with it. It was rudely broken

11

by the harsh voice of the traitor now for the first time
giving utterance to his secret heartlessness and malice.
"To what purpose is this waste?" (Matt. 26:8b) The
unjust steward with his impious economy making up for
his own private thefts by grudging honor to his Master.
Thus in the midst of the sweet calm harmony of that
feast at Bethany, there comes a jar and discord: all is
wrong: sour discontent and distrust are spreading, for
the devil is abroad.

Judas, having once shown what he was, lost no time
in carrying out his malice. He went to the Chief Priests
and bargained with them to betray his Lord for a price.
Our Lord saw all that took place within him; He saw
Satan knocking at his heart, and admitted there and
made an honored and beloved guest and an intimate.
He saw him go to the priests and heard the conversation
between them. He had seen it by His foreknowledge all
the time he had been about Him, and when He chose
him. What we faintly know has to be, affects us far
more vividly and very differently when it actually takes
place. Our Lord had at length felt, and allowed Himself to feel, the cruelty of the ingratitude of which He
was the sport and victim. He had treated Judas as one
of His most familiar friends. He had shown marks of the
closest intimacy; He had made him the purse-keeper of
Himself and His followers. He had given him the power
of working miracles. He had admitted him to a
knowledge of the mysteries of the kingdom of heaven.
He had sent him out to preach and made him one of His
own special representatives, so that the Master was
judged by the conduct of His servant. A heathen, when
smitten by a friend, said, "Et tu, Brute!" "And you,
Brutus!" What desolation is in the sense of ingratitude!
God who is met with ingratitude daily cannot from His
divine nature feel it. He took a human heart, that He

might feel it in its fullness. And now, O my God, though in heaven, dost Thou not feel my ingratitude towards Thee?

I see the figure of a man, whether young or old I cannot tell. He may be fifty or He may be thirty. Sometimes He looks one, sometimes the other. There is something inexpressible about His face which I cannot solve. Perhaps, as He bears *all* burdens, He bears that of old age, too. But so it is; His face is at once most venerable, yet most childlike, most calm, most sweet, most modest, beaming with sanctity and with lovingkindness. His eyes rivet me and move my heart. His breath is all fragrant, and transports me out of myself. Oh, I will look upon that Face for ever and will not cease.

And I see suddenly someone come to Him, and raise his hand and sharply strike Him on that heavenly face. It is a hard hand, the hand of a rude man, and perhaps has iron upon it. It could not be so sudden as to take Him by surprise who knows all things past and future, and He shows no sign of resentment, remaining calm and grave as before; but the expression of His face is marred; a great weal arises, and in a little time that all-gracious Face is hid from me by the effects of this indignity, as if a cloud came over It.

A hand was lifted up against the Face of Christ. Whose hand was that? My conscience tells me: "thou art the man." I trust it is not so with me now. But, O my soul, contemplate the awful fact. *Imagine* Christ before thee, and *imagine* thyself lifting up thy hand and striking Him! Thou wilt say, "It is impossible: I could not do so." Yes, thou hast done so. When thou didst sin willfully, then thou hast done so. He is beyond pain now: still thou hast struck Him, and had it been in the days of His flesh, He would have felt pain. Turn back in memory and recollect the time, the day, the hour,

when by willful sin, by scoffing at sacred things, or by
profaneness, or by dark hatred of this thy brother, or by
acts of impurity, or by deliberate rejection of God's
voice, or in any other devilish way known to thee, thou
hast struck the All-holy One.

PRAYER

O injured Lord, what can I say? I am very guilty
concerning Thee, my Brother; and I shall sink in sullen
despair if Thou dost not raise me. I cannot look on
Thee. I shrink from Thee; I throw my arms around my
face; I crouch to the earth. Satan will pull me down if
Thou take not pity. It is terrible to turn to Thee; but
oh, turn Thou me, and so shall I be turned. It is a
purgatory to endure the sight of Thee, the sight of
myself — I, who am most vile, Thou who art most
holy. Yet make me look once more on Thee whom I
have so incomprehensively affronted, for Thy countenance is my only life. My only hope and health lies in
looking on Thee whom I have pierced. So I put myself
before thee; I look on Thee again; I endure the pain in
order to receive the purification.

O my God, how can I look Thee in the Face when I
think of my ingratitude, so deeply seated, so habitual,
so immovable — or rather so awfully increasing! Thou
loadest me day by day with Thy favors, and feedest me
with Thyself, as Thou didst Judas, yet I not only do not
profit thereby, but I do not even make any acknowledg-
ment at the time. Lord, how long? when shall I be free
from this real, this fatal captivity? He who made Judas
his prey has got foothold of me in my old age, and I
cannot get loose. It is the same day after day. When
wilt Thou give me a still greater grace than Thou hast
given, the grace to profit by the graces which Thou
givest? When wilt Thou give me Thy effectual grace

which alone can give life and vigor to this effete, miserable, dying soul of mine? My God, I know not in which sense I can pain Thee in Thy glorified state; but I know that every fresh sin, every fresh ingratitude I now commit, was among the blows and stripes which once fell on Thee in Thy passion. O let me have as little share in those Thy past sufferings as possible. Day by day goes, and I find that I have been more and more, by the new sins of each day, the cause of them. I know that at best I have a real share *in solido* of them all, but still it is shocking to find myself having a greater and greater share. Let others wound Thee — let not me. Let me not have to think that Thou wouldst have had this or that pang of soul or body the less, except for me. O my God, I am so fast in prison that I cannot get out.

THE SYMPATHY OF JESUS, MARY AND JOSEPH[1]

Sympathy may be called an eternal law, for it is signified or rather transcendentally and archetypically fulfilled in the ineffable mutual love of the Divine Trinity. God, though infinitely One, has ever been Three. He ever has rejoiced in His Son and His Spirit, and they in Him — and thus through all eternity He has existed, not solitary, though alone, having in this incomprehensible multiplication of Himself and reiteration of His Person, such infinitely perfect bliss, that

---

[1] Two of Webster's definitions of *sympathy*: 1. An affinity, association, or relationship between things so that whatever affects one, similarly affects the other or others; mutual or reciprocal susceptibility; hence, a reaction or response brought about by such relationship. 2. Reciprocal liking and understanding arising from community of interests, aims, etc., and compatibility of temperaments.

nothing He has created can add aught to it. The devil only is barren and lonely, shut up in himself— and his servants also.

When, for our sakes, the Son came on earth and took our flesh, yet He would not live without the sympathy of others. For thirty years He lived with Mary and Joseph and thus formed a shadow of the Heavenly Trinity on earth. Oh, the perfection of that sympathy which existed between the three! Not a look of one, but the other two understood, as expressed, better than if expressed in a thousand words — nay more than understood, accepted, echoed, and corroborated. It was like three instruments absolutely in tune which all vibrate when one vibrates, and vibrate either one and the same note, or in perfect harmony.

The first weakening of that union was when Joseph died. It was no jar in the sound, for to the last moment of his life he was one with them, and the sympathy between the three only became more intense and more sweet while it was brought into new circumstances and had a wider range in the months of his declining, his sickness, and death. Then it was like an air ranging through a number of notes performed perfectly and exactly in time and tune by all three. But it ended in a lower note than before, and when Joseph went, a weaker one. Not that Joseph, though saintly, added much in volume of sound to the other two, but sympathy, by its very meaning, implies number, and, on his death, one of the three harps was unstrung and silent.

Oh, what a moment of sympathy between the three, the moment before Joseph died — they supporting and hanging over him, he looking at them and reposing in them with undivided, unreserved, supreme devotion, for he was in the arms of God and the Mother of God. As a flame shoots up and expires, so was the ecstasy of that last moment ineffable, for each knew and thought of the reverse which was to follow on the snapping of that bond. One moment, very different, of joy, not of sorrow, was equal to it in intensity of feeling, that of the birth of Jesus. The birth of Jesus, the death of Joseph, moments of unutterable sweetness, unparallelled in the history of mankind. After Joseph's death, Jesus had to preach, suffer and die; Mary to witness His sufferings, and even after He had risen again, to go on living without Him amid the changes of life and the heartlessness of the heathen.

The birth of Jesus, the death of Joseph, those moments of transcendentally pure and perfect and living sympathy between the three members of the earthly Trinity, were its beginning and its end. The death of Joseph, which broke it up, was the breaking up of more than itself. It was but the beginning of that change which was coming over Son and Mother. Going on now for thirty years, each of them had been preserved from the world and had lived for each other. Now He had to go out to preach and suffer, and, as the foremost and most inevitable of His trials, and one which from first to last He voluntarily undertook, even when not imperative, He deprived Himself of the enjoyment of that intercommunion of hearts — of His heart with the heart of Mary — which had been His from the time He took man's nature, and which He had possessed in an archetypal and transcendent manner with His Father and His Spirit from all eternity.

MEDITATION AND PRAYER

O my soul, thou art allowed to contemplate this union of the three, and to share thyself its sympathy, by faith though not by sight. My God, I believe and know that then a communion of heavenly things was opened

on earth which has never been suspended. It is my duty
and my bliss to enter into it myself. It is my duty and
my bliss to be in tune with that most touching music
which then began to sound. Give me that grace which
alone can make me hear and understand it, that it may
thrill through me. Let the breathings of my soul be with
Jesus, Mary and Joseph. Let me live in obscurity, out of
the world and the world's thought with them. Let me
look to them in sorrow and in joy, and live and die in
their sweet sympathy.

OUR LORD REFUSES SYMPATHY

The *last* day of the earthly intercourse between Jesus
and Mary was at the marriage feast at Cana. Yet even
then there was something taken from that blissful intimacy, for they no longer lived simply for each other,
but showed themselves in public, and began to take
their place in the dispensation which was opening. He
manifested forth His glory by His first miracle; and hers
also, by making her intercession the medium of it.
He honored her still more by breaking through the
appointed order of things for her sake, and though His
time of miracles was not come, anticipating it at her
request. While He wrought His miracle, however, He
took leave of her, in the words, "Woman, what is
between thee and Me?" Thus He parted with her absolutely, though He parted with a blessing. It was leaving Paradise feeble and alone.

For in truth it was fitting that He who was to be the
true High Priest, should thus, while He exercised His

office for the whole race of man, be free from all human ties and sympathies of the flesh. And one reason for His long abode at Nazareth with His Mother may have been to show, that, as He gave up His Father's and His own glory on high to become man, so He gave up the innocent and pure joys of His earthly home, in order that He might be a Priest. So, in the old time, Melchisedech is described as without father or mother. So the Levites showed themselves truly worthy of the sacerdotal office and were made the sacerdotal tribe, because they steeled themselves against natural affection, said to father or mother, "I know you not," and raised the sword against their own kindred when the honor of the Lord of Hosts demanded the sacrifice. In like manner our Lord said to Mary, "What is between Me and thee?" It was the setting apart of the sacrifice, the first ritual step of the Great Act which was to be solemnly performed for the salvation of the world. "What is between Me and thee, O woman?" is the offertory before the oblation of the Host. O my dear Lord, Thou who hast given up Thy Mother for me, give me grace cheerfully to give up all my earthly friends and relations for Thee.

The Great High Priest said to His kindred, "I know you not." Then, as He did so, we may believe that the most tender heart of Jesus looked back upon His whole time since His birth, and called before Him those former days of His infancy and childhood, when He had been with others from whom He had long been parted. Time was when St. Elizabeth and the Holy Baptist had formed part of the Holy Family. St. Elizabeth, like St. Joseph, had been removed by death, and was waiting His coming to break that bond which detained both her and St. Joseph from Heaven. St. John had been cut off from his home and mankind, and from the sympathies of earth long since — and had now begun to preach the coming Savior, and was waiting and expecting His manifestation.

PRAYER

Give me grace, O Jesus, to live in sight of that blessed company. Let my life be spent in the presence of Thee and Thy dearest friends. Though I see them not, let not what I do see seduce me to give my heart elsewhere. Because Thou hast blessed me so much and given to me friends, let me not depend or rely or throw myself in any way upon them, but in Thee be my life, and my conversation and daily walk among those with whom Thou didst surround Thyself on earth, and dost now delight Thyself in Heaven. Be my soul with Thee, and because with Thee, with Mary and Joseph and Elizabeth and John.

WITH MARY

Let us linger for a while with Mary — before we follow the steps of her Son, our Lord. There was an occasion when He refused permission to one who would bid His own home farewell, before he followed Him. And such was, as it seems, almost His own way with His Mother. But will He be displeased, if we one instant stop with her, though our meditation lies with Him? O Mary, we are devoted to your seven woes, but was not this, though not one of those seven, one of the greatest, and included those that followed, from your knowledge of them beforehand? How did you bear that first separation from Him? How did the first days pass when thou wast desolate? Where didst thou hide thyself? Where didst thou pass the long three years and more, while He was on His ministry? Once — at the beginning of it — thou didst attempt to get near Him, and then we hear nothing of thee till we find thee standing at His cross. And then, after that great joy of seeing Him again, and the permanent consolation, never to be lost, that with Him all suffering and humiliation was over, and that never had she to weep for Him again, still she was separated from Him for many years, while she lived in the flesh, surrounded by the wicked world, and in the misery of His absence.

The blessed Mary, among her other sorrows, suffered the loss of her Son, after He had lived under the same roof with her for thirty years. When he was no more than twelve, He gave her a token of what was to be, and said, "I must be about My Father's business." And when the time came, and He began His miracles, He said to her, "What have you to do with me?" (John 2:4). What is common to us two? — and soon He left her. Once she tried to see Him, but in vain, and could not reach Him for the crowd, and He made no effort to receive her, nor said a kind word; and then at last, once more she tried, and she reached Him in time to see Him hanging on the cross and dying. He was only forty days on earth after the resurrection, and then He left her in old age to finish her life without Him. Compare her thirty happy years and her time of desolation.

I see her in a forlorn home, while her Son and Lord was going up and down the land without a place to lay His head, suffering both because she was so desolate and He was so exposed. How drearily passed the day; and then came reports that He was in some peril or distress. She heard, perhaps, that He had been led into the wilderness to be tempted. She would have shared all His sufferings, but was not permitted. Once there was a profane report which was believed by many, that He was beside Himself, and His friends and kindred went out to get possession of Him. She went out, too, to see Him and tried to reach Him. She could not for the crowd. A message came to Him to that effect, but He made no effort to receive her, nor said a kind word. She went back to her home disappointed, without the sight of Him. And so she remained, perhaps in company with those who did not believe in Him.

I see her too after His ascension. This, too, is a time of bereavement, but still of consolation. It was still a twilight time, but not a time of grief. The Lord was absent, but He was not on earth, He was not in suffering. Death had no power over Him. And He came to her day by day in the Blessed Sacrifice. I see the Blessed Mary at Mass, and St. John celebrating. She is waiting for the moment of her Son's Presence. Now she converses with Him in the sacred rite; and what shall I say now? She receives Him to whom once she gave birth.

O Holy Mother, stand by me now at Mass time, when Christ comes to me, as thou didst minister to thy infant Lord — as thou didst hang upon His words when He grew up, as thou wast found under His cross. Stand by me, Holy Mother, that I may gain somewhat of thy purity, thy innocence, thy faith, and He may be the one object of my love and my adoration as He was of thine.

BETRAYED, DESERTED, DENIED

There were others who more directly ministered to Him, and of whom we are told more — the Holy Angels. It was the voice of the Archangel that announced to the prophet His coming which consigned the Eternal to the womb of Mary. Angels hymned His nativity and all the Angels of God worshipped at His crib. An Angel sent Him into Egypt and brought Him back. Angels ministered to Him after His temptation. Angels wrought His miracles when He did not will to exert His Almighty fiat. But He bade them go at length, as He had bidden His Mother go. One remained at His agony. Afterwards He said, "Think ye not that I could pray to My Father, and He would send Me myriads of Angels?" — implying that in fact His guards had been withdrawn. The Church prays Him, on His ascension, "King of Glory, Lord of Angels, leave us not orphans." He, the Lord of Angels, was at this time deprived of them.

He took other human friends when He had given up His Mother — the twelve Apostles — as if He desired that in which He might sympathize. He chose them, as He says, to be "not servants, but friends." He made them His confidants. He told them things which He did not tell others. It was His will to favor, nay, to indulge them, as a father behaves toward a favorite child. He made them more blessed than kings and prophets and wise men, from the things He told them. He called them "His little ones," and preferred them for His gifts to the wise and prudent. He exulted, while He praised them, that they had continued with Him in His temptations, and as if in gratitude He announced that they should sit upon twelve thrones judging the twelve tribes of Israel. He rejoiced in their sympathy when His solemn trial was approaching. He assembled them about Him at the Last Supper, as if they were to support Him in it. "With desire," He says, "have I desired to eat this Passover with you before I suffer." Thus there was an interchange of good offices, and an intimate sympathy between them. But it was His adorable will that they too should leave Him, that He should be left to Himself. One betrayed, another denied Him, the rest ran away from Him, and left Him in the hands of His enemies. Even after He had risen, none would believe it. Thus He trod the winepress alone.

He who was Almighty and All-blessed, who flooded His own soul with the full glory of the vision of His divine nature, would still subject that soul to all the infirmities which naturally belonged to it. And, as He allowed it to rejoice in the sympathy, and to be desolated under the absence of human friends, so, when it pleased Him, He could, and did, deprive it of the light of the presence of God. This was the last and crowning misery that He put upon it. He had in the course of His ministry fled from man to God. He had appealed to Him. He had taken refuge from the rude ingratitude of the race whom He was saving in divine communion. He retired at night to pray. He said, "the Father loveth the Son, and shows Him all things that He doth Himself." He returned thanks to Him for hiding His mysteries from the wise to reveal them to the little ones. But now He deprived Himself of this elemetary consolation, by which He lived, and that, not in part only, but in its fullness. He said, when His Passion began, "My soul is sorrowful even unto death"; and at the last, "My God, why hast Thou forsaken Me?" Thus He was stripped of all things.

PRAYER

My God and Savior, who wast thus deprived of the light of consolation, whose soul was dark, whose affections were left to thirst without the true object of them, and all this for man, take not from *me* the light of Thy countenance, lest I shrivel from the loss of it and perish in my infirmity. Who can sustain the loss of the Sun of the soul but Thou? Who can walk without light, or labor without the pure air, but Thy great Saints? As for me, alas, I shall turn to the creature for my comfort, if Thou wilt not give me Thyself. I shall not mourn, I shall not hunger or thirst after justice, but I shall look about for whatever is at hand, and feed on refuse, or stay my appetite with husks, ashes, or chaff, which if they poison me not, at least nourish not.

O my God, leave me not in that dry state in which I am; give me the comfort of Thy grace. How can I have any tenderness or sweetness, unless I have Thee to look upon? How can I continue in prayer as is my duty, . . . unless Thou encourage me and make it pleasant for me? It is hardly that an old man keeps any warmth in him; it is but slowly that he recovers what is lost.

THE BODILY SUFFERINGS OF OUR LORD

His bodily pains were greater than those of any martyr, because He willed them to be greater. All pain of body depends, as to be felt at all, so to be felt in this or that degree, on the nature of the living mind which dwells in that body. Vegetables have no feeling because they have no living mind or spirit within them. Brute animals feel more or less according to the intelligence within them. Man feels more than any brute, because he has a soul; Christ's soul felt more than that of any other man, because His soul was exalted by personal union with the Word of God. Christ felt bodily pain more keenly than any other man, as much as man feels pain more keenly than any other animal.

It is a relief to pain to have the thoughts drawn another way. Thus, soldiers in battle often do not know when they are wounded. Again, persons in raging fevers seem to suffer a great deal; then afterwards they can but recollect general discomfort and restlessness. And so excitement and enthusiasm are great alleviations of bodily pain; thus savages die at the stake, amid torments, singing songs; it is a sort of mental drunkenness. And so again, an instantaneous pain is comparatively bearable; it is the continuance of pain which is so heavy, and if we had no memory of the pain we suffered the minute before, which we also suffer in the present, we should find pain easier to bear; but what makes the second pang grievous is that there has been a first pang. And what makes the third more grievous is that there has been a first and second; the pain seems to grow because it is prolonged. Now Christ suffered, not as in delirium or in excitement, or in inadvertency, but He looked pain in the face! He offered his whole mind to it, and received it, as it were, directly into His bosom, and suffered all He suffered with full consciousness of suffering.

Christ would not drink the drugged cup which was offered to Him to cloud His mind. He willed to have the full sense of pain. His soul was so intently fixed on His suffering as not to be distracted from it; and it was so active and so recollected the past and anticipated the future, that the whole passion was, as it were, concentrated in each moment of it. All that He had suffered and all that He was to suffer lent its aid to increase what He was suffering. Yet withal His soul was so calm and sober and unexcited as to be passive, and thus to receive the full burden of the pain in it, without the power of throwing it from Himself. Moreover, the sense of conscious innocence, and the knowledge that His sufferings would come to an end, might have supported Him; but He repressed the comfort and turned His thoughts away from these alleviations that He might suffer absolutely and perfectly.

PRAYER

O my God and Savior, who went through such sufferings for me with such lively consciousness, such precision, such recollection, and such fortitude, enable me, by Thy help, if I am brought into the power of this terrible trial, bodily pain, enable me to bear it with some portion of Thy calmness.

THE SORROW OF HIS SOUL

Our Lord's sufferings were so great, because His soul was in suffering. What shows this is that His soul began to suffer before His bodily passion, as we see in the agony in the garden. The first anguish which came upon His body was not from without — it was not from the scourges, the thorns, or the nails, but from His soul.

His soul was in such agony that He called it death. "My soul is sorrowful even unto death." The anguish was such that it, as it were, burst open His whole body. It was a pang affecting His heart; as in the deluge the floods of the great deep were broken up and the windows of heaven were open. The blood, rushing from His tormented heart, forced its way on every side, formed for itself a thousand new channels, filled all the pores, and at length stood forth upon His skin in thick drops, which fell heavily on the ground.

He remained in this living death from the time of His agony in the garden; and as His first agony was from His soul, so was His last. As the scourge and the cross did not begin His sufferings, so they did not close them. It was the agony of His soul, not of His body, which caused His death. His persecutors were surprised to hear that He was dead. How, then, did He die? That agonized, tormented heart, which at the beginning so awfully relieved itself in the rush of blood and the bursting of His pores, at length broke. It broke and He died. It would have broken *at once*, had He not kept it from breaking. At length the moment came. He gave the word and His heart broke.

PRAYER

O tormented Heart, it was love, and sorrow, and fear, which broke Thee. It was the sight of human sin, it was the sense of it, the feeling of it laid on Thee; it was zeal for the glory of God, horror at seeing sin so near Thee, a sickening, stifling feeling at its pollution, the deep shame and disgust and abhorrence and revolt which it inspired, keen pity for the souls whom it had drawn headlong into hell — all these feelings together Thou didst allow to rush upon Thee. Thou didst submit

Thyself to their powers, and they were Thy death. That strong Heart, that all-noble, all-generous, all-tender, all-pure Heart was slain by sin.

O most tender and gentle Lord Jesus, when will my heart have a portion of Thy perfections? When will my hard and stony heart, my proud heart, my unbelieving, my impure heart, my narrow, selfish heart, be melted and conformed to Thine? O teach me so to contemplate Thee that I may become like Thee, and to love Thee sincerely and simply as Thou hast loved me.

IT IS CONSUMMATED
A Meditation at the End of Lent

It is over now, O Lord, as with Thy sufferings, so with our humiliations. We have followed Thee from Thy fasting in the wilderness till Thy death on the Cross. For forty days we have professed to do penance. The time has been long and it has been short; but whether long or short, it is now over. It is over and we feel a pleasure that it is over; it is a relief and a release. We thank Thee that it is over. We thank Thee for the time of sorrow, but we thank Thee more as we look forward to the time of festival. Pardon our shortcomings in Lent and reward us in Easter.

PRAYER

We have, indeed, done very little for Thee, O Lord. We remember well our listlessness and weariness; our indisposition to mortify ourselves when we had no plea of health to stand in the way; our indisposition to pray and to meditate — our disorder of mind, our discontent, our peevishness. Yet some of us, perhaps, have done something for Thee. Look on us as a whole, O Lord, look on us as a community, and let what some have done well plead for us all.

O Lord, the end is come. We are conscious of our languor and lukewarmness; we do not deserve to rejoice in Easter, yet we cannot help doing so. We feel more of pleasure, we rejoice in Thee more than our past humiliation warrants us in doing; yet may that very joy be its own warrant. Oh, be indulgent to us, for the merits of Thine own all-powerful Passion. Accept us as Thy little flock in the day of small things, in a fallen country, in an age when faith and love are scarce. Pity us and spare us and give us peace.

O my own Savior, now in the tomb but soon to arise, Thou hast paid the price; it is done — *consummatum est* — it is secured. Oh, fulfill Thy resurrection in us, and as Thou hast purchased us, claim us, take possession of us, make us Thine.

GOD AND THE SOUL

GOD AND THE BLESSEDNESS OF THE SOUL

To possess Thee, O Lover of souls, is happiness, and the only happiness of the immortal soul! To enjoy the sight of Thee is the only happiness of eternity. At present I might amuse and sustain myself with the vanities of sense and time, but they will not last forever. We shall be stripped of them when we pass out of this world. All shadows will one day be gone. And what shall I do then? There will be nothing left to me but the Almighty God. If I cannot take pleasure in the thought of Him, there is no one else then to take pleasure in; God and my soul will be the only two beings left in the whole world as far as I am concerned. He will be all in all, whether I wish it or not. What a strait I shall then be in if I do not love Him, and there is then nothing else to love! if I feel averse to Him, and He is then ever looking upon me!

Ah, my dear Lord, how can I bear to say that Thou wilt be all in all whether I wish it or not? Should I not wish it with my whole heart? What can give me happiness but Thou? If I had all the resources of time and sense about me, just as I have now, should I not in the course of ages, nay of years, weary of them? If this world should last forever, would it ever be able to supply my soul with food? Is there any earthly thing which I do not weary of at length even now? Do old men love what young men love? Is there not constant change? I am sure then, my God, that the time would come, though it might be long in coming, when I should have exhausted all the enjoyment which the world could give. Thou alone, my dear Lord, art the food for eternity, and Thou alone. Thou only canst satisfy the soul of man. Eternity would be misery without Thee, even though Thou didst not inflict punishment. To see Thee, to gaze on Thee, to contemplate Thee, this alone is inexhaustible. Thou indeed are unchangeable, yet in Thee there are always more glorious depths and more varied attributes to search into. We shall ever be beginning as if we had never gazed upon Thee. In Thy Presence are torrents of delight, which whoso tastes will never let go. This is my true portion, O my Lord, here and hereafter!

My God, how far am I from acting according to what I know so well! I confess it, my heart goes after shadows. I love anything better than communion with Thee. I am ever eager to get away from Thee. Often I find it difficult even to say my prayers. There is hardly any amusement I would not rather take up than set myself to think of Thee. Give me grace, O my Father, to be utterly ashamed of my own reluctance! Rouse me from sloth and coldness, and make me desire Thee with my whole heart. Teach me to love meditation, sacred reading, and prayer. Teach me to love that which must engage my mind for all eternity.

JESUS CHRIST YESTERDAY AND TODAY, AND THE SAME FOREVER

All things change here below. I say it, Lord; I believe it; and I shall feel it more and more the longer I live. Before Thine eyes, most awesome Lord, the whole future of my life lies bare. Thou knowest exactly what will befall me every year and every day till my last hour. And, though I know not what Thou seest concerning me, this much I know, that Thou dost read in my life perpetual change. Not a year will leave me as it found me, either within or without. I shall never remain any length of time in one state. How many things are sure to happen to me, unexpected, sudden, hard to bear! I know them not. I know not how long I have to live. I am hurried on, whether I will it or not, through continual change. O my God, what can I trust in? There is nothing I dare trust in; nay, did I trust in anything of earth, I believe for that very reason it would be taken away from me. I know Thou wouldst take it away, if Thou hadst love for me.

Everything short of Thee, O Lord, is changeable, but Thou endurest. Thou art ever one and the same. Ever the true God of man, and unchangeably so. Thou art the rarest, most precious, the sole good; and withal Thou art the most lasting. The creature changes, the Creator never. Then only the creature stops changing, when it rests on Thee. On Thee the Angels look and are at peace; that is why they have perfect bliss. They never can lose their blessedness, for they never can lose Thee. They have no anxiety, no misgivings — because they love the Creator; not any being of time and sense, but "Jesus Christ, the same yesterday and today, who is also forever."

My Lord, my only God, my God and my all, let me never go after vanities. "Vanity of vanities; all is vanity." All is vanity and shadow here below. Let me not give my heart to anything here. Let nothing allure me from Thee. Oh, keep me wholly and entirely. Keep Thou this most frail heart and this most weak head in Thy Divine keeping. Draw me to Thee morning, noon and night for consolation. Be Thou my own bright Light, to which I look for guidance and peace. Let me love Thee, O my Lord Jesus, with a pure affection and a fervent affection! Let me love Thee with the fervor, only greater, with which men of this earth love beings of this earth. Let me have that tenderness and constancy in loving Thee, which is so much praised among men, when the object is of the earth. Let me find and feel Thee to be my only joy, my only refuge, my only strength, my only comfort, my only hope, my only fear, my only love.

AN ACT OF LOVE

My Lord, I believe and know and feel that Thou art the Supreme Good. And, in saying so, I mean, not only supreme Goodness and Benevolence, but that Thou art the sovereign and transcendent Beautifulness. I believe that, beautiful as is Thy creation, it is mere dust and ashes and of no account, compared with Thee, who art the infinitely more beautiful Creator. I know well, that therefore it is that the Angels and Saints have such perfect bliss, because they see Thee. To see even the glimpse of Thy true glory, even in this world, throws holy men into an ecstasy. And I feel the truth of all this, in my own degree, because Thou hast mercifully taken our nature upon Thee, and hast come to me as man. "And we beheld His glory, the glory as it were of the only begotten of the Father." The more, O my dear Lord, I meditate on Thy words, works, actions, and sufferings in the Gospel, the more wonderfully glorious and beautiful I see Thee to be.

And therefore, O my dear Lord, since I perceive Thee to be so beautiful, I love Thee, and desire to love Thee more and more. Since Thou art the One Goodness, Beautifulness, Gloriousness, in the whole world of being, and there is none like Thee, but Thou art infinitely more glorious and good than even the most beautiful of creatures, therefore I love Thee with a singular love, a one and only sovereign love. Everything, O my Lord, shall be dull and dim to me after looking at Thee. There is nothing on earth, not even what is most naturally dear to me, that I can love in comparison to Thee. And I would lose everything whatever rather than lose Thee. For Thou, O my Lord, art my supreme and only Lord and love.

My God, Thou knowest infinitely better than I, how little I love Thee. I should not love Thee at all except for Thy grace. It is Thy grace which has opened the eyes of my mind, and enabled them to see Thy glory. It is Thy grace which has touched my heart, and brought upon it the influence of what is so wonderfully beautiful and fair. How can I help loving Thee, O my Lord, except by some dreadful perversion, which hinders me from looking at Thee? O my God, whatever is nearer to me than Thou, things of this earth and things more naturally pleasing to me, will be sure to interrupt the sight of Thee unless Thy grace interfere. Keep Thou my eyes, my ears, my heart, from any such miserable tyranny. Break my bonds — raise my heart. Keep my whole being fixed on Thee. Let me never lose sight of Thee; and while I gaze on Thee, let my love of Thee grow more and more every day.

AGAINST THEE ONLY HAVE I SINNED

Thou, O Lord, after living a whole eternity in ineffable bliss, because Thou art the one and sole Perfection, at length didst begin to create spirits to be with Thee and to share Thy blessedness according to their degree; and the return they made Thee was at once to rebel against Thee. First a great part of the Angels, then mankind, have risen up against Thee, and served others, not Thee. Why didst Thou create us, but to make us happy? Couldest Thou be made more happy by creating us? And how could we be happy but in obeying Thee? Yet we determined not to be happy as Thou wouldest have us happy, but to find out a happiness of our own; and so we left Thee. O my God, what a return is it that we — that I — make Thee when we sin! What dreadful unthankfulness is it! And what will be my punishment for refusing to be happy, and for preferring hell to heaven! I know what the punishment will be: Thou wilt say, "Let him have it all his own way. He wishes to perish. Let him perish. He despises the graces I give him; they shall turn to a curse."

Thou, O my God, hast a claim on me, and I am wholly Thine! Thou art the Almighty Creator, and I am Thy workmanship. I am the work of Thy Hands, and Thou art my Owner. As well might the axe or the hammer exalt itself against its framer, as I against

Thee. Thou owest me nothing. I have no rights in respect to Thee, I have only duties. I depend on Thee for life, and health, and every blessing every moment. I have no more power of exercising will as to my life than axe or hammer. I depend on Thee far more entirely than anything here depends on its owner and master. The son does not depend on the father for the continuance of life — the matter out of which the axe is made existed first — but I depend wholly on Thee — if Thou withdraw Thy breath from me for a moment, I die. I am wholly and entirely Thy property and Thy work, and my one duty is to serve Thee.

O my God, I confess that before now I have utterly forgotten this, and that I am continually forgetting it! I have acted many a time as if I were my own master, and turned from Thee rebelliously. I have acted according to my own pleasure, not according to Thine. And so far have I hardened myself, as not to feel as I ought how evil this is. I do not understand how dreadful a sin it is — and I do not hate it and fear it as I ought. I have no horror of it, or loathing. I do not turn from it with indignation, as being an insult to Thee, but I trifle with it, and even if I do not commit great sins, I have no great reluctance to do small ones. O my God, what a great and awful difference there is between what I am and what I ought to be!

SIN AND GRACE

My God, I dare not offend any earthly superior; I am afraid — for I know I shall get into trouble — yet I dare offend Thee. I know, O Lord, that, according to the greatness of the person offended against, the greater is the offence. Yet I do not fear to offend Thee, whom to offend is to offend the infinite God. O my dear Lord, how should I myself feel, what should I say of myself, if I were to strike some revered superior on earth? If I were violently to deal a blow upon someone as revered as a father or a priest, if I were to strike them on the face? I cannot bear even to think of such a thing — yet what is this compared with the lifting up of my hand against Thee? And what is sin but this? To sin is to insult Thee in the grossest of all conceivable ways. This then, O my soul, is what the sinfulness of sin consists in! It is the lifting up of my hand against my Infinite Benefactor, against my Almighty Creator, Preserver and Judge — against Him in which all majesty and glory and beauty and reverence and sanctity center; against the one and only God.

O my God, I am utterly confounded to think of the state in which I lie! What will become of me if Thou art severe? What is my life, O my dear and merciful Lord, but a series of offences, little or great, against Thee? O what great sins I have committed against Thee before now — and how continually in lesser matters I am sinning! My God, what will become of me? What will be my position hereafter if I am left to myself? What can I do but come humbly to Him whom I have so heavily affronted and insulted, and beg Him to forgive the debt which lies against me? O my Lord Jesus, whose love for me has been so great as to bring Thee down from heaven to save me, teach me, dear

Lord, my sin — teach me its heinousness — teach me truly to repent of it — and pardon it in Thy great mercy!

I beg Thee, O my dear Savior, to recover me! Thy grace alone can do it. I cannot save myself. I cannot recover my lost ground. I cannot turn to Thee, I cannot please Thee, or save my soul without Thee. I shall go from bad to worse, I shall fall from Thee entirely, I shall quite harden myself against my neglect of duty, if I rely on my own strength. I shall make myself my center instead of making Thee. I shall worship some idol of my own framing instead of Thee, the only true God and my Maker, unless Thou hinder it by Thy grace. O my dear Lord, hear me! I have lived long enough in this undecided, wavering, unsatisfactory state. I wish to be Thy good servant. I wish to sin no more. Be gracious to me and enable me to be what I know I ought to be.

THE EFFECTS OF SIN

My Lord, Thou art the infinitely merciful God. Thou lovest all things that Thou hast created. Thou art the lover of souls. How then is it, O Lord, that I am in a world so miserable as this can be? Can this be the world which Thou has created, so full of pain and suffering? Who among the sons of Adam lives without suffering from his birth to his death? How many bad sicknesses and diseases there are! How many frightful accidents! How many great anxieties! How are men brought down and broken by grief, distress, the tumult of passions and continual fear! What dreadful plagues there ever are on this earth: war, famine, and pestilence! Why is this, O my God? Why is this, O my soul? Dwell upon it, and ask thyself, Why is this? Has God changed His nature? Yet how evil has the earth become!

O my God, I know full well why all these evils are. Thou hast not changed Thy nature, but man has ruined his own. We have sinned, O Lord, and this is the cause of this change. All these evils which I see and in which I partake are the fruit of sin. They would not have been, had we not sinned. They are but the first installment of the punishment of sin. They are an imperfect and dim image of what sin is. Sin is infinitely worse than famine, war and pestilence. Take the most hideous of diseases, under which the body wastes away and corrupts, the blood is infected; the head, the heart, the lungs, every organ disordered, the nerves unstrung and shattered; pain in every limb, thirst, restlessness, delirium — all is nothing compared with that dreadful sickness of the soul which we call sin. They all are the effects of it, they all are shadows of it, but nothing more. That cause itself is something different in kind, is of a malignity far different and far greater than all these things. O my God, teach me this! Give me to understand the enormity of that evil under which I labor and know it not. Teach me what sin is.

All these dreadful pains of body and soul are the fruits of sin, but they are nothing to its punishment in the world to come. The keenest and fiercest of bodily pains is nothing to the fire of hell; the most dire horror or anxiety is nothing to the never-dying worm of conscience; the greatest bereavement, loss of substance, desertion of friends, and forlorn desolation is nothing compared to the loss of God's countenance. Eternal punishment is the only true measure of the guilt of sin. My God, teach me this. Open my eyes and heart, I earnestly pray Thee, and make me understand how awful a body of death I bear about me. And, not only teach me about it, but in Thy mercy and by Thy grace remove it.

THE EVIL OF SIN

My God, I know that Thou didst create the whole universe very good; and if this was true of the material world which we see, much more true is it of the world of rational beings. The innumerable stars which fill the firmament, and the very elements out of which the earth is made, all are carried through their courses and their operations in perfect concord; but much higher was the concord which reigned in heaven when the Angels were first created. At that first moment of their existence the main orders of the Angels were in the most excellent harmony, and beautiful to contemplate; and the creation of man was expected next, to continue that harmony in the instance of a different kind of being. Then it was that suddenly was discovered a flaw or a rent in one point of this most delicate and exquisite web — and it extended and unravelled the web, till a third part of it was spoilt; and then again a similar flaw was found in human kind, and it extended over the whole race. This dreadful evil, destroying so large a portion of all God's works, is sin.

My God, such is sin in Thy judgment; what is it in the judgment of the world? A very small evil or none at all. In the judgment of the Creator it is that which has marred His spiritual work; it is a greater evil than though the stars got loose, and ran wild in heaven, and chaos came again. But man, who is the guilty one, calls it by soft names. He explains it away. The world laughs at it and is indulgent to it; and, as to its deserving eternal punishment, it rises up indignant at the idea, and rather than admit it, would deny the God who has said it does deserve such. The world thinks sin the same sort of imperfection as an impropriety, or lack of taste or as an infirmity. O my soul, consider carefully the great difference between the views of sin taken by Almighty God and the world! Which of the two views do you mean to believe?

O my soul, which of the two wilt thou believe — the Word of God or the word of man? Is God right, or is the creature right? Is sin the greatest of all possible evils or the least? My Lord and Savior, I have no hesitation which to believe. Thou art true, and every man a liar. I will believe Thee above the whole world. My God, imprint on my heart the infamous deformity of sin. Teach me to abhor it as a pestilence — as a fierce flame destroying on every side; as my death. Let me take up arms against it and devote myself to fight under Thy banner in overcoming it.

THE HEINOUSNESS OF SIN

My Lord, I know well that Thou art all perfect and needest nothing. Yet I know that Thou hast taken upon Thyself the nature of man, and, not only so, but in that nature didst come upon earth and suffer all manner of evil and didst die. This is a history which has hung the heavens with sackcloth, and taken from this earth, beautiful as it is, its light and glory. Thou didst come, O my dear Lord, and Thou didst suffer in no ordinary way, but unheard-of and extreme torments! The all-blessed Lord suffered the worst and most various of pains. This is the corner truth of the Gospel. It is the one foundation: Jesus Christ and Him Crucified. I know it, O Lord. I believe it and I put it steadily before me.

Why is this strange anomaly in the face of nature? Does God do things for nothing? No, my soul, it is sin. It is thy sin which has brought the Everlasting down upon the earth to suffer. Hence I learn how great an evil sin is. The death of the Infinite is its sole measure. All that slow distress of body and mind which He endured from the time He shed His blood at Gethsemane down to His death, all that pain came from sin. What sort of evil is that, which had to be so encountered by such a sacrifice, and to be reversed at such a price! Here then I understand best how horrible a thing sin is. It is horrible, because through it have come upon men all those evils whatever they are, with which the earth abounds. It is more horrible, in that it has nailed the Son of God to the accursed tree.

My dear Lord and Savior, how can I make light of that which has had such consequences! Henceforth I will, through Thy grace, have deeper views of sin than before. Fools make jest of sin, but I will view things in their true light. My suffering Lord, I have made Thee suffer. Thou art most beautiful in Thy eternal nature, O my Lord. Thou art most beautiful in Thy sufferings! Thy adorable attributes are not dimmed, but increased to us as we gaze on Thy humiliation. Thou art more beautiful to us than before. But still I will never forget that it was man's sin, my sin, which made that humiliation necessary. *Amor meus crucifixus est* — "my Love is crucified," but by none other than me. I have crucified Thee, my sin has crucified Thee. O my Savior, what a dreadful thought — but I cannot undo it. All I can do is to hate that which made Thee suffer. Shall I not do that at least? Shall I not love my Lord just so much as to hate that which is so great an enemy of His, and break off all terms with it? Shall I not put off sin altogether? By Thy great love of me, teach me and enable me to do this, O Lord. Give me a deep-rooted, intense hatred of sin.

THE BONDAGE OF SIN

Thou, O my Lord and God, Thou alone art strong. Thou alone art holy! Thou art the *Sanctus Deus, Sanctus fortis* — "Holy God, Holy and strong." Thou art the sanctity and the strength of all things. No created nature has any stay or subsistence in itself, but crumbles and melts away if Thou art not with it to sustain it. My God, Thou art the strength of the Angels, of the Saints in glory — of holy men and women on earth. No being has any sanctity or any strength apart from Thee. My God, I wish to adore Thee as such. I wish with all my heart to understand and to confess this great truth, that not only art Thou Almighty, but that there is no might at all, or power, or strength, anywhere but in Thee.

My God, if Thou art the strength of all spirits, O how pre-eminently art Thou my strength! O how true it is, so that nothing is more so, that I have no strength but in Thee! I feel intimately, O my God, that whenever I am left to myself, I go wrong. As sure as a stone falls down to the earth if it be let go, so surely my heart and spirit fall down hopelessly if they are let go by Thee. Thou must uphold me by Thy right hand, or I cannot stand. How strange it is, but how true, that all my natural tendencies are towards sloth, towards excess, towards neglect of religion, towards neglect of prayer, towards love of the world, not towards love of Thee, or love of sanctity, or love of self-governance. I approve and praise what I do not do. My heart runs after vanities, and I tend towards death, I tend to corruption and dissolution, apart from Thee, *Deus immortalis.*

My God, I have had enough experience of what a dreadful bondage sin is. If Thou art absent, I find I cannot keep myself, however I wish it — and am in the hands of my own self-will, pride, sensuality and selfishness. And they prevail with me more and more every day, till they are irresistible. In time the old Adam within me gets so strong that I become a mere slave. I confess things to be wrong which nevertheless I do. I bitterly lament over my bondage, but I cannot undo it. O what a tyranny is sin! It is a heavy weight which cripples me — and what will be the end of it? By Thy all-precious merits, by Thy Almighty power, I intreat Thee, O my Lord, to give me life and sanctity and strength. *Deus sanctus*, give me holiness! *Deus fortis*, give me strength! *Deus immortalis*, give me perseverance. *Sanctus Deus, Sanctus fortis, Sanctus immortalis*, have mercy on us![1]

---

[1] This ancient prayer is found in both Greek and Latin in the Good Friday Service.

CALLED TO PERFECTION

I do not wish to frighten imperfect Christians, but to lead them on; to open their minds to the greatness of the work before them, to dissipate the meager and carnal view in which the Gospel has come to them, to warn them that they must never be contented with themselves or stand still and relax their efforts, but must go on *unto perfection*; to warn them further that till they are much more than they are at present, they have received the kingdom of God in word, not in power; that they are not spiritual persons, and can have no comfortable sense of Christ's presence in their souls.

What is it, then, that they lack? Several passages of Scripture which will make it plain. "If any man be in Christ, he is a new creature: old things are passed away; behold, all things are become new." (II Cor. 5:17) "The life which I now live in the flesh I live by the faith of the Son of God, who loved me, and gave Himself for me." (Gal. 2:20) "The love of Christ constraineth us." (II Cor. 5:14) "Put on, therefore, as the elect of God, holy and beloved, bowels of mercies, kindness, humbleness of mind, meekness, longsuffering, forbearing one another, and forgiving one another, if any man have a quarrel against any, even as Christ forgave you, so also do ye; and above all these things, put on charity, which is the bond of perfectness. And let the peace of God rule in your hearts, to the which also ye are called in one body, and be ye thankful. Let the word of Christ dwell in you richly in all wisdom." (Col. 3:12-16) "God hath sent forth the Spirit of His Son into your hearts." (Gal. 4:6). Lastly, our Savior's own memorable words, "If any man will come after Me, let him deny himself, and take up his cross daily, and follow Me." (Luke 9:23).

Now it is plain that this is a very different mode of obedience from any which natural reason and conscience tells us of — different, not in its nature, but in its excellence and peculiarity. It is much more than honesty, justice, and temperance; and *this* is to be a Christian. Observe how it is different from that lower degree of religion which we may possess without entering into the mind of the Gospel.

First of all it is different in its faith, which is placed, not simply in God, but in God as manifested in Christ according to His own words: "You believe in God; believe also in Me." (John 14:1). Next, we must adore Christ as our Lord and Master and love Him as our most gracious Redeemer. We must have a deep sense of our guilt and of the difficulty of securing heaven; we must live as in His presence, daily pleading His cross and passion, thinking of His holy commandments, imitating His sinless pattern, and depending on the gracious aids of His Spirit; that we may really and truly be servants of Father, Son and Holy Spirit, in whose name we were baptized.

Further, we must, for His sake, aim at a noble and unusual strictness of life, perfecting holiness in His fear, destroying our sins, mastering our whole soul, and bringing it into captivity to His law, denying ourselves lawful things in order to do Him service, exercising a profound humility, and an unbounded, never-failing love, giving away much of our substance in religious and charitable works, and discountenancing and shunning irreligious men. This is to be a Christian — a gift easily described and in a few words, but attainable only with fear and much trembling; promised, indeed, and in a measure accorded at once to everyone who asks for it, but not secured till after many years, and never in this life fully realized.

But be sure of this, that every one of us who has had the opportunities of instruction and sufficient time, and yet does not in some good measure possess it, every one, who, when death comes, has not gained his portion of that gift which it requires a course of years to gain, and which he might have gained, is in a peril so great and fearful that I do not like to speak about it. As to the notion of a partial and ordinary fulfillment of duties of honesty, industry, sobriety and kindness "availing" him, it has no Scriptural encouragement. We must stand or fall by another and higher rule. We must become what St. Paul calls "new creatures"; that is, we must have lived and worshipped God as the redeemed of Jesus Christ, in all faith and humbleness of mind, in reverence towards His Word and ordinances, in thankfulness, in resignation, in mercifulness, gentleness, purity, patience and love.

How evident it is that we are far from the kingdom of God! Let each in his own conscience apply this to himself. Here is a thought not to keep us from rejoicing in the Lord Christ, but to make us "rejoice with trembling," (Psalm 2:11) wait diligently on God, pray Him earnestly to teach us more of our duty, and to impress the love of it on our hearts.

From *Plain and Parochial Sermons*, Vol. I.(abridged).

JESUS THE LAMB OF GOD

Behold the Lamb of God, behold Him who taketh away the sins of the world. So spoke St. John the Baptist when he saw our Lord coming to him. And in so speaking, he did but appeal to that title under which our Lord was known from the beginning. Just so, Abel showed forth his faith in Him by offering of the firstlings of his flock. Abraham, in place of his son Isaac whom God spared, offered the like for a sacrifice. The Israelites were enjoined to sacrifice once a year, at Easter time, a lamb — one lamb for each family, a lamb without blemish — to be eaten whole, all but the blood, which was sprinkled, as their protection, about their house doors. The Prophet Isaiah speaks of our Lord under the same image: "He shall be led as a sheep to the slaughter, and shall be dumb as a lamb before his shearers." (Isa. 53:7). And all this because "He was wounded for our iniquities, He was bruised for our sins; . . . by His stripes we are healed."(verse 5). And in like manner the holy Evangelist St. John, in the visions of the Apocalypse, thus speaks of Him: "I saw, . . . and behold a Lamb standing as it were slain"; and then he saw all the blessed "fall down before the Lamb," and they sang a new song saying, "Thou wast slain, and hast redeemed us to God by Thy blood out of every tribe and tongue and people and nation". . . "Worthy is the Lamb that was slain, to receive power and wealth and wisdom and strength, and honor and glory and blessing." (Rev. 5:6, 8,9 and 12).

This is Jesus Christ, who when darkness, sin, guilt and misery had overspread the earth, came down from heaven, took our nature upon Him, and shed His precious blood upon the Cross for all men.

Let us pray for all nations, that they may be converted.

O Lord Jesus Christ, O King of the whole world, O
Hope and Expectation of all nations, O Thou who hast
bought all men for Thine own at the price of Thy most
precious blood, look down in pity upon all races who
are spread over the wide earth, and impart to them the
knowledge of Thy truth. Remember, O Lord, Thine
own most bitter sufferings of soul and body in Thy
betrayal, Thy passion and Thy crucifixion, and have
mercy upon their souls. Behold, O Lord, but a portion
of mankind has heard of Thy Name — and yet thousands
upon thousands in the East and the West, in the North
and the South, hour after hour, as each hour comes, are
dropping away from this life into eternity. Remember,
O my dear Lord, and lay it to heart, that to the dis-
honor of Thy Name and to the triumph of Thy enemies,
fresh victims are choking up the infernal pit, and are
taking up their dwelling there for ever. Listen to the
intercessions of Thy saints, let Thy Mother plead with
Thee, let not the prayers of Thy Church be offered up
in vain. Impute not to the poor heathen their many
sins, but vist the earth quickly and give all men to
know, to believe, and to serve Thee, in whom is our
salvation, life, and resurrection, who with the Father
liveth and reigneth in the unity of the Holy Spirit, one
God for ever and ever. Amen.

JESUS THE SON OF DAVID

Our Lord asked the Pharisees, saying, "What think ye of Christ? Whose son is He?" They said unto Him, "The Son of David." For so the Prophet Isaiah had foretold: "There shall come forth a rod out of the root of Jesse." Jesse was the father of David, the King of the Jews, and by "rod" or plant is meant the Blessed Virgin. "There shall come forth a rod out of the root of Jesse, and a flower shall rise up out of his root." (Isa. 11:1). By the flower of the plant is meant our Lord, the Son of the Blessed Mary. "And the Spirit of the Lord shall rest upon Him"(verse 2). This the Holy Spirit did at His Baptism. And Jeremiah says, "Behold the days come, and I will raise up to David a just Branch and a King shall reign, and shall be wise, and shall execute judgment and justice in the earth. In those days Judah shall be saved . . . and this is the name that they shall call Him — the Lord our Just One." (Jer. 23:5-6) Hence the Jews, when disputing whether our Lord were the Christ, said, "Doth not the Scripture say that Christ cometh out of the seed of David?" (John 7:42).

It was the glory of the Jews that the promised Savior, the Christ, the Sacrifice and Propitiation for the whole human race, the Almighty Liberator, was to be of their race and country. Yet, dreadful to say, when He came, they rejected Him. "He came unto His own, and His own received Him not." (John 1:11).

Let us pray for the Jewish nation, that they may turn to the Lord their God.

O seed of Abraham, O Son of David, O Adonai and leader of the House of Israel, who didst appear to Moses in the burning bush and didst on Mount Sinai deliver to him Thy Law; O Key of David, and Sceptre of the

House of Israel, who openest and no one shutteth, who shuttest and no one openeth; visit not, O dear Lord, the sins of the fathers upon the children. Spare this poor nation which was once so high in Thy sight, and now hath fallen so low. O remember not those old priests and scribes, the Pharisees and Saducees, remember not Annas and Caiphas, Judas, and the insane multitude who cried, "Crucify Him." In Thy wrath remember mercy. Forgive their obstinacy and forgive their impenitence — forgive their blindness to things spiritual and their avowed love of this world and its enjoyments. Touch their hearts and give them true faith and repentance. Have mercy, O Jesus, on Thine own brethren — have mercy on the countrymen of Thy Mother, of St. Joseph, of Thy apostles, of St. Paul, of Thy great saints, Abraham, Moses, Samuel and David. O Lord, hear: O Lord, be appeased: O Lord, hearken and do not delay for Thine own sake, O my God, for Thy Name was once named upon the city Jerusalem and Thy people. (Dan. 9:19).

JESUS THE LORD OF GRACE

When our Lord was rejected by His own country, the Jews, He chose other nations instead of them. Thus the Holy Evangelist, after saying, "He came unto His own, and His own received Him not," adds, "But to as many as received Him, to them He gave power to be made the sons of God, to them that believe in His name; who are born, not of blood, nor of the will of the flesh, nor of the will of man, but of God." (John

1:11-13). That is, provided that men believed in Him, whatever was their race or country, He made them His sons and gave them the gifts of grace and the promise of heaven. He had warned the Jews of this before their time of grace was over. "I say unto you," He said, "that the kingdom of God shall be taken from you, and shall be given to a nation bringing forth the fruits thereof." (Matt. 21:43). And hence St. Paul, His great Apostle, when he found the Jews would not listen to him, when they "gainsaid and blasphemed," shook his garments and said, "Your blood be upon your own heads; I am clean; from henceforth I will go unto the Gentiles." (Acts 18:6). And if God cast off His own people, the Jews, so much more will He cast off any other people who cast Him off. Hence the same St. Paul says, "If some branches (that is, the Jews) be broken (off), and thou (that is, a man of some other nation) art ingrafted in them (instead), and art made partaker of the root and of the fatness of the olive tree; boast not . . . . Because of unbelief they were broken off; but thou standest by faith; be not high-minded, but fear. For if God hath not spared the natural branches, *fear* lest He spare not thee." This misery has happened to this country, to our own England. God chose it and blessed it for nearly a thousand years; it rebelled, lost faith, and He cast it off out of His Church.

Let us pray for the recovery of our own country [England] to the faith and the Church of Christ.

O Sapientia, O Wisdom who hast issued out of the mouth of the Highest, and reachest in Thy Providence from the beginning to the end of all things, and disposest all things in sweetness and in strength, it was by Thy unmerited grace, we acknowledge it, O Lord, that this country of ours was so many centuries ago brought into the true fold and gifted with the knowledge of Thy truth and the grace of Thy Sacraments. Alas! how things have changed since then! The people was small and of little account; now it stands highest among the nations of the earth. Then it was obscure and poor — now it has amazing wealth and pre-eminent power. But then it was great in Thy sight, and now on the contrary, it is little, for it has lost Thee. O my God, what doth it profit though we gain the whole world and lose our own souls? or what exchange shall we give for our souls? Wilt Thou forget, O Lord, what by Thy grace we once were, before we turned from Thee? Wilt Thou not listen to all our Saints and Martyrs who are now reigning with Thee and are ever interceding for us? O look not upon our haughtiness and pride; look not upon our impurity; but look upon Thine own merits; look upon the wounds in Thy hands; look upon Thy past mercies towards us; and in spite of our willfulness, subdue our hearts to Thee, O Savior of men, and renew Thy work in the midst of the years, in the midst of the years re-establish Thou it.

JESUS THE AUTHOR AND FINISHER OF FAITH

St. Paul tells us to "look on Jesus, the Author and Finisher of faith." Faith is the first step towards salvation, and without it we have no hope. For St. Paul says, "Without faith it is impossible to please God." It is a divine light; by it we are brought out of the darkness into sunshine; by it, instead of groping, we are able to

see our way towards heaven. Moreover, it is a great *gift*
which comes from above, and which we cannot obtain
except from Him who is the object of it. He, our Lord
Jesus Himself, and He alone, gives us the grace to
believe in Him. Hence the Holy Apostle calls Him the
Author of our faith — and He finishes and perfects it
also — from first to last it is altogether from Him.
Therefore it was that our Lord said, "If thou canst
believe, all things are possible to him that believeth."
(Mark 9:23). And hence the poor man to whom He
spoke, who believed indeed already, but still feebly,
made answer — "crying out with tears, I *do* believe,
Lord; help Thou my unbelief." Hence, too, on another
occasion, the Apostles said to our Lord, "Increase our
faith." (Luke 17:5). And St. Paul draws out fully the
whole matter when he reminds his converts, "And you
hath He raised, when you were dead in your trespasses
and sins, wherein in time past you walked, following
the course of this world, . . . in which we all walked in
time past, . . . and were by nature children of wrath,
even as the rest; but God, who is rich in mercy, out of
the great love wherewith He loved us, even when we
were dead in sins, hath quickened us together in Christ.
By grace you are saved through faith, and this is not of
yourselves, for it is the gift of God." (Eph. 2:1-8).

*Let us pray for all the scorners, scoffers and unbelievers,
all false teachers and opposers of truth.*

O Lord Jesus Christ, upon the Cross Thou didst say,
"Father forgive them for they know not what they do."
And this surely, O my God, is the condition of vast
multitudes among us now; they know not what they
might have known, or they have forgotten what they
once knew. They deny that there is a God, but they
know not what they are doing. They laugh at the joys

of heaven and the pains of hell, but they know not what they are doing. They renounce all faith in Thee, the Savior of man, they despise Thy Word and Sacraments, they revile and slander Thy holy Church, but they know not what they are doing. They mislead the wandering, they frighten the weak, they corrupt the young, but they know not what they do. Others, again, have a wish to be religious, but mistake error for truth — they go after fancies of their own and they seduce others to keep them from Thee. They know not what they are doing, but Thou canst make them know. O Lord, we urge Thee by Thine own dear words, "Lord and Father, forgive them, for they know not what they do." Teach them now, open their eyes here, before the future comes; give them faith in what they must see hereafter, if they will not believe in it here. Give them a full and saving faith here; destroy their dreadful delusions, and give them to drink of that living water, which whoso hath shall not thirst again.

JESUS THE LORD OF HOSTS

Among the visions which the beloved disciple St. John was given to see, and which he has recorded in his Apocalypse, one was that of our Lord as the Commander and Leader of the hosts of the Saints in their warfare with the world. "I saw," he says, "and behold a white horse, and He that sat on him had a bow, and there was a crown given Him; and He went forth conquering that He might conquer." (Rev. 6:2). And again, "I saw heaven opened, and behold a white horse, and

He that sat upon him was called Faithful and True, and with justice doth He judge and fight." . . . And He was clothed with a garment sprinkled with blood, and His Name is called, *The Word of God.* And the armies that are in heaven followed Him on white horses, clothed in fine linen, white and clean." (Rev. 19: 11, 13). Such is the Captain of the Lord's Host, and such are His soldiers. He and they ride on white horses, which means that their cause is innocent and pure. Warriors of this world wage *unjust* wars, but our Almighty Leader fights for a heavenly cause and with heavenly weapons — and in like manner His soldiers fight the good fight of faith; they fight against their and their Master's three great enemies — the World, the Flesh, and the Devil. He is covered with blood, but it is His own blood which He shed for our redemption. And His followers are red with blood, but still again it is His blood, for it is written, "They have washed their robes and have made them white in the blood of the Lamb." (Rev. 7:14). And again, He and they are certain of victory because it is said, "He went forth conquering that He might conquer." (Rev. 6:2). So let us say with the Psalmist, "Gird Thy sword upon Thy thigh, O Thou most mighty, for the cause of truth and meekness and justice Thy right hand shall teach Thee dread deeds." (Psalm 45:3 and 4b).

Let us pray for the whole Church Militant here upon earth.

O Lion of the Tribe of Judah, the root of David, who fightest the good fight, and hast called on all men to join Thee, give Thy courage and strength to all Thy soldiers over the whole earth, who are fighting under the standard of Thy Cross. Give grace to everyone in his own place to fight Thy battle well. Be with Thy missionaries in pagan lands, put right words into their mouths, prosper their labors, and sustain them under their sufferings with Thy consolations, and carry them on, even through torments and blood (if it be necessary), to their reward in heaven. Give the grace of wisdom to those in high station, that they may neither yield to fear, nor be seduced by flattery. Make them prudent as serpents, and simple as doves. Give Thy blessing to all preachers and teachers, that they may speak Thy words and persuade their hearers to love Thee. Be with all faithful servants, whether in low station or in high, who mix in the world; instruct them how to speak and how to act every hour of the day, so as to preserve their own souls from evil and to do good to their companions and associates. Teach us, one and all, to live in Thy presence and to see Thee, our Great Leader, and Thy Cross — and thus to fight valiantly and to overcome, that at the last we may sit down with Thee in Thy Throne, as Thou hast overcome and art set down with Thy Father on His Throne.

JESUS THE ONLY BEGOTTEN SON

Jesus is the only Son of the only Father — as it is said in the Creed, "I believe in one God, the Father Almighty," and then "and in Jesus Christ, His only Son our Lord." And so He Himself says in the Gospel, "As the Father has life in Himself, so He hath given to the Son also to have life in Himself." (John 5:26). And He said to the man whom he cured of blindness, "Dost thou believe in the Son of God? It is He that talketh with thee." (John 9:35-37). And St. John the Evangelist says, "The Word was made flesh and dwelt among us, and we saw His glory, the glory as it were of the only-begotten of the Father." (John 1:14). And St. John the Baptist says, "The Father loveth the Son and He hath given all things into His hand. He that believeth in the Son hath life everlasting." (John 3:35,36). And St. Paul says, "There is one body and one Spirit — as ye are called in one hope of your calling. One Lord, one faith, one baptism, one God and Father of all." (Eph. 4:4-6).

Thus Almighty God has set up *all* things in unity — and therefore His Holy Church in a special way, as the Creed again says, "One Holy Catholic and Apostolic Church." It is His wise and gracious will that His followers should not follow their own way and form many bodies, but one. This was the meaning of the mystery of His garment at the time of His crucifixion which "was without seam, woven from the top throughout." (John 19:23). And therefore it was that the soldiers were not allowed to break His sacred limbs, for like the Jewish Passover Lamb, not a bone of Him was to be broken.

Let us pray for the unity of the Church and the reconciliation and peace of all Christians.

O Lord Jesus Christ, who, when Thou wast about to suffer, didst pray for Thy disciples to the end of time that they might all be one, as Thou art in the Father and the Father in Thee: look down in pity on the manifold divisions among those who profess Thy faith, and heal the many wounds which the pride of man and the craft of Satan have inflicted upon Thy people. Break down the walls of separation which divide one party and denomination of Christians from another.... As there is but one holy company in heaven above, so likewise may there be but one communion, confessing and glorifying Thy holy Name here below.

JESUS THE ETERNAL KING

Our Lord was called Jesus when He took flesh of the Blessed Virgin. The Angel Gabriel said to her, "Behold, thou shalt bring forth a Son, and thou shalt call His name Jesus." But though He then gained a new name, He had existed from eternity. He never was not — He never had a beginning — and His true name, therefore, is the Eternal King. He ever reigned with His Father and the Holy Spirit, three Persons, one God. And hence, shortly before His crucifixion, He said, "Glorify Thou me, O Father, with Thyself, with the glory which I had before the world was, with Thee." (John 17:5). He who was the eternal King in heaven, came to be King, and Lord, and Lawgiver, and Judge upon earth. Hence the prophet Isaiah says, foretelling His coming, "A Child is born to us, and a Son is given to us, and the government is upon His shoulder; and His name shall be called Wonderful, Counsellor, God the Mighty, the Father of the world to come, the Prince of Peace." (Isaiah 9:6). And when He left the world, He left His power behind Him, and divided it among His followers. He gave one portion of His power to one, another to another. He gave the fullness of His power to St. Peter and to his successors, who, in consequence, are His vicars and representatives — so that, as the Father sent the Son, so the Son has sent St. Peter. But not only St. Peter and the other Apostles, but all bishops and prelates in Thy Church, all pastors of souls, all Christian kings have power from Him, and stand to us in His place.

Let us pray for all Rulers in the Church.

O Emmanuel, God with us, who art the Light that enlightenth all men, who from the time when Thou camest upon earth hast never left it to itself; who after teaching Thy Apostles, gave them to teach others to succeed them, and didst especially leave St. Peter and his successors... to guide and rule us in Thy stead age after age, till the end come....We believe and confess, O Lord, without any hesitation at all, that Thou hast promised a continuous duration to Thy Church while the world lasts — and we confess before Thee that we are in no doubt or trouble whatever, we have not a shadow of misgiving as to the permanence and the spiritual well-being either of Thy Church itself or of its rulers. We do not know what is best for Thy Church, or for the interests of the Catholic faith... throughout the world at this time.[1] We leave the event entirely to Thee; we do so without any anxiety, knowing that everything must turn to the prosperity of Thy ransomed possession.

[1]Probably written at the time when the Pope was about to lose control of the Church States, a territory stretching across mid-Italy from sea to sea, comprising an area of 16,000 square miles. The Bishops of Rome were first given rule of this territory in 754, but it had been subject to the rivalries of conflicting forces and alliances. In 1859, the territory was reduced to a mere 4,891 square miles, but even this was eyes as fair game by revolutionaries under Garabaldi, and by Victor Emmanuel II, king of Italy. In October, 1870, the states of the church were incorporated with Italy, and in 1871, Rome became the seat of government. A law that year guaranteed the Pope possession of the Vatican and Lateran palaces, the villa of Catel Gandolfo, and an annual income of 3,225,000 francs forever. Pope Pius IX and his successors considered themselves prisoners in the Vatican until a concordat was signed between Pope Pius XI and Mussolini in 1929, making Vatican City a separate state with full temporal power, and making further adjustments of financial affairs.

JESUS THE BEGINNING OF
THE NEW CREATION

Our Lord Jesus Christ is said by His almighty power to have begun a new creation, and to be Himself the firstfruit and work of it. Mankind was lost in sin, and was thereby, not only not an heir of heaven, but a slave of the evil one. Therefore He who made Adam in the beginning resolved in His mercy to make a new Adam, and by a further ineffable condescension determined that that new Adam should be Himself. And therefore, by his holy prophet Isaiah, He announced before He came, "Behold I create new heavens and a new earth." (Isaiah 65:17) On the other hand, St. Paul calls Him "The image of the invisible God, the first-born of every creature." (Col. 1:15) And St. John calls Him "the Amen, the faithful and true witness, who is the beginning of the creation of God." (Rev. 3:14). The Creator came as if He were a creature because He took upon Him a created nature — and as, at the first, Eve was formed out of the side of Adam, so now, when He hung on the cross, though not a bone of Him was broken, His side was pierced, and out of it came the grace, represented by the blood and the water, out of which His bride and spouse, His Holy Church, was made. And thus all the sanctity of all portions of that Holy Church is derived from Him as a beginning; and He feeds us with His divine Flesh in the Holy Eucharist, in order to spread within us, in the hearts of all of us, the blessed leaven of the New Creation. All the wisdom of the Doctors, and the courage and endurance of the Martyrs, and the purity of Virgins, and the zeal of Preachers, and the humility and mortifications of religious men are from Him, as the beginning of the new and heavenly creation of God.

Let us pray for all ranks and conditions of men in the Church.

O Lord, who art called the Branch, the Orient, the Splendor of the eternal light, and the Sun of Justice, who art that Tree of whom Thy beloved disciple speaks as the Tree of life, bearing twelve fruits, and its leaves for the healing of the nations, give Thy grace and blessing on all those various states and conditions in Thy Holy Church which have sprung from Thee and live in Thy life. Give to all Bishops the gifts of knowledge, discernment, prudence and love. Give to all priests to be humble, tender and pure; give to all pastors of Thy flock to be zealous, vigilant, and unworldly; give to all religious bodies to act up to their rule, to be simple and without guile, and to set their hearts upon invisible things and them only. Grant to fathers of families to recollect that they will have hereafter to give account of the souls of their children; grant to all husbands to be tender and true; to all wives to be obedient and patient; grant to all children to be docile; to all young people to be chaste; to all the aged to be fervent in spirit; to all who are engaged in business to be honest and unselfish; and to all of us the necessary graces of faith, hope, charity and contrition.

JESUS THE LOVER OF SOULS

The inspired writer says, "Thou hast mercy upon all because Thou canst do all things, and overlookest the sins of men for the sake of repentance. For Thou lovest all things that are, and hatest none of the things which

Thou hast made. . . . And how could anything endure, if Thou wouldst not? or be preserved if not called by Thee? But Thou sparest all, because they are Thine, O Lord, who lovest souls." (Wisdom 11:24-27). This is what brought Him from Heaven and gave Him the name, Jesus — for the angel said to St. Joseph about Mary, "She shall bring forth a Son, and thou shalt call His name Jesus; for He shall save His people from their sins." (Matthew 1:21). It was His great love for souls and compassion for sinners which drew Him from heaven. Why did He consent to veil His glory in mortal flesh, except that He desire so much to save those who had gone astray and lost all hope of salvation? Hence He says Himself, "The Son of Man is come to seek and to save that which was lost." (Matthew 17:11, Luke 19:10). Rather than that we should perish, He did all that even omnipotence could do consistently with its holy attributes, for He gave Himself. And He loves each of us so much that He has died for each one as fully and absolutely as if there were no one else for Him to die for. He is our best Friend, our true Father, the only real Lover of our souls — He takes all means to make us love Him in return, and He refuses us nothing if we do.

Let us pray for the conversion of all sinners.

O Lord, who didst give Thyself for us, that Thou mightest redeem us from all iniquity, and mightest purify to Thyself "a people acceptable, zealous for good works" (Titus 2:14), look upon Thy baptized, look on the multitude of those who once were Thine and have gone from Thee. Ah, for how short a time do they keep Thy grace in their hearts, how soon do they fall off from Thee, with what difficulty do they return! And even though they repent and come to penance, yet how soon, in the words of Scripture, doth the dog return to his vomit, and the sow that was washed to her wallowing in the mire! O my God, save us all from the seven deadly sins, and rescue those who have been made captive by them. Convert all sinners — bring judgments down upon them if there is no other way of reclaiming them. Touch the hearts of all proud men, wrathful, revengeful men, of the obstinate, of the self-relying, of the envious, of the slanderer, of the hater of goodness and truth; of the slothful and torpid; of all gluttons and drunkards; of the covetous and unmerciful; of all licentious talkers; of all who indulge in impure thoughts, words or deeds. Make them understand that they are going straight to hell, and save them from themselves and from Satan.

JESUS OUR GUIDE AND GUARDIAN

There are men who think that God is so great that He disdains to look down upon *us*, our doings and our fortunes. But He who did not find it beneath His majesty to make us, does not think it beneath Him to observe and to visit us. He says Himself in the Gospel: "Are not five sparrows sold for two farthings? and not one of them is forgotten before God. Yea, the very hairs of your head are all numbered. Fear not, therefore: you are of more value than many sparrows." (Luke 12:6) He determined from all eternity that He would create us. He settled our whole fortune — and, if He did not absolutely decree to bring us to heaven, it is because we have free will, and by the very constitution of our nature He has put it in part out of His own power, for we must do *our* part if to heaven we attain. But He has done everything short of this. He died for us all upon the Cross, that, if it were possible to save us, we might be saved. And He calls upon us lovingly, begging us to accept the benefit of His meritorious and most precious Blood. And those who trust Him He takes under His special protection. He marks out their whole life for them; He appoints all that happens to them; He guides them in such a way as to secure their salvation; He gives them just so much of health, of wealth, of friends, as is best for them; He afflicts them only when it is for their good; He is never angry with them. He measures out just that number of years which is good for them; and He appoints the hour of their death in such a way as to secure their perseverance to it.

Let us pray for ourselves and for all our needs.

O my Lord and Savior, in Thy arms I am safe; keep me and I have nothing to fear; give me up and I have nothing to hope for. I know not what will come upon me before I die. I know nothing about the future, but I rely upon Thee. I pray Thee to give me what is good for me; I pray Thee to take from me whatever may imperil my salvation. I pray Thee not to make me rich, I pray Thee not to make me very poor; but I leave it all to Thee, because Thou knowest and I do not. If Thou bringest pain or sorrow on me, give me grace to bear it well — keep me from fretfulness and selfishness. If Thou givest me health and strength and success in this world, keep me ever on my guard lest these great gifts carry me away from Thee. O Thou who didst die on the Cross for me, even for me, sinner as I am, give me to know Thee, to believe on Thee, to love Thee, to serve Thee; ever to aim at setting forth Thy glory; to live to and for Thee; to set a good example to all around me; give me to die just at that time and in that way which is most for Thy glory, and best for my salvation.

JESUS SON OF MARY

When our Lord came upon earth, He might have created a fresh body for Himself out of nothing — or He might have formed a body for Himself out of the earth as He formed Adam. But He preferred to be born, as other men are born, of a human mother. Why did He do so? He did so to put honor on all those earthly relations and connections which are ours by nature; and to teach us that though He has begun a new creation, He does not wish us to cast off the old creation, as far as it is not sinful. Hence it is our duty to love and honor our parents, to be affectionate to our brothers, sisters, friends, husbands, wives, not only less, but even more, than it was man's duty before our Lord came on earth.

As we become better Christians, more consistent and zealous servants of Jesus, we shall become only more and more anxious for the good of all around us — our kindred, our friends, our acquaintances, our neighbors, our superiors, our inferiors, our masters, our employers. And this we shall do by recalling how our Lord loved His Mother. He loves her still in heaven with a special love. He refuses her nothing. We then on earth must feel a tender solicitude for all our relations, all our friends, all whom we know or have dealings with. And, moreover, we must love not only those who love us, but those who hate us or injure us, that we may imitate Him who not only was loving to His Mother, but even allowed Judas, the traitor, to kiss Him, and prayed for His murderers on the Cross.

Let us pray God for our relations, friends, well wishers, and enemies, living and dead.

O Jesus, Son of Mary, whom Mary followed to the Cross when Thy disciples fled, and who didst bear her tenderly in mind in the midst of Thy sufferings, even in Thy last words; who didst commit her to Thy best beloved disciple, saying to her, "Woman, behold thy son," and to him, "Behold thy mother," we after Thy pattern would pray for all who are near and dear to us, and we beg Thy grace to do so continually. We beg Thee to bring them all into the light of Thy truth, or keep them in Thy truth if they already know it, and to keep them in a state of grace, and to give them the gift of perseverance. We thus pray for our parents, our fathers and our mothers, for our children, for every one of them, for our brothers and sisters, for every one of our brothers and every one of our sisters, for our cousins and all our kindred, for our friends — for all our old friends, for our dear and intimate friends, for our teachers, for our pupils, for our masters and employers, for those who serve us, for our associates and fellow-workers, for our neighbors, for our superiors and rulers; for those who wish us well, for those who wish us ill; for our enemies; for our rivals; for our injurers and for our slanderers. And not only for the living but for the dead who have died in the grace of God, that He may . . . admit them into His presence above.

JESUS OUR DAILY SACRIFICE

Our Lord not only offered Himself as a Sacrifice on the Cross, but He makes Himself a perpetual, a daily sacrifice to the end of time. In the Holy Eucharist, that One Sacrifice on the Cross once offered is renewed, continued, applied to our benefit. He seems to say, My Cross was raised up 1800 years ago, and only for a few hours — and very few of My servants were present there — but I intend to bring millions into My Church. For their sakes then I will perpetuate my Sacrifice, so that each of them may be as though they had severally been present on Calvary. I will offer Myself up day by day to the Father, that every one of My followers may have the opportunity to offer his petitions to Him, sanctified and recommended by the all-meritorious virtue of My passion. Thus I will be a Priest forever, after the order of Melchisedech — My priests shall stand at the altar, but not they, but I rather will offer. I will not let them offer mere bread and wine, but I Myself will be present upon the Altar instead, and I will offer up Myself invisibly while they perform the outward rite. And thus the Lamb that was slain once for all, though He is ascended on high, ever remains a victim from His miraculous presence in Holy Mass under the figure and appearance of mere earthly and visible symbols.

Let us pray for all who day by day have calls upon us.

My Lord Jesus Christ, Thou hast given me this great gift, that I am allowed not only to pray for myself, but to intercede for others in Thy holy Mass. Therefore, O Lord, I pray Thee to give all grace and blessing upon this town and every inhabitant of it — upon Thy Church in it, for our bishop and his clergy, and for all catholic places of worship and their congregations. I pray Thee to bless and prosper all the good works and efforts of all priests, religious and all Thy faithful people. I pray for all the sick, all the suffering, all the poor, all the oppressed — I pray for all prisoners — I pray for all evil doers. I pray for all ranks in the community — I pray for the Queen and Royal Family — for the Houses of Parliament — for the judges and magistrates — for all our soldiers — for all who defend us in ships — I pray for all who are in peril or danger. I pray for all who have benefited me, befriended me, or aided me. I pray for all whom I have forgotten; Bring us all after all the troubles of this life into the haven of peace, and reunite us together for ever, O my dear Lord, in Thy glorious heavenly kingdom.

THE POWER OF THE CROSS

O my God, who could have imagined by any light of nature, that it was one of Thy attributes to lower Thyself and to work out Thy purposes by Thine own humiliation and suffering? Thou hadst lived from eternity in ineffable blessedness. My God, I might have understood as much as this, *viz.*, that when Thou didst begin to create and surround Thyself with a world of creatures, that these attributes would show themselves in Thee which before had no exercise. Thou couldest not show Thy power when there was nothing whatever to exercise it. Then too, Thou didst begin to show Thy wonderful and tender providence, Thy faithfulness, Thy solicitous care for those whom Thou hadst created. But who could have fancied that Thy creation of the universe implied and involved in it Thy humiliation? O my great God, Thou hast humbled Thyself, Thou hast stooped to take our flesh and blood, and hast been lifted up upon the tree! I praise and glorify Thee tenfold the more, because Thou hast shown Thy power by means of Thy suffering, than hadst Thou carried on Thy work without it. It is worthy of Thine infinitude thus to surpass and transcend all our thoughts.

O my Lord Jesu, I believe, and by Thy grace will ever believe and hold, and I know that it is true and will be true to the end of the world, that nothing great is done without suffering, without humiliation, and that all things are possible by means of it. I believe, O my God, that poverty is better than riches, pain better than pleasure, obscurity and contempt than name, and ignominy and reproach than honor. My Lord, I do not ask Thee to bring these trials upon me, for I know not if I could face them; but at least, O Lord, whether I be in prosperity or adversity, I will believe that it is as I have said. I will never have faith in riches, rank, power or reputation. I will never set my heart on worldly success or on worldly advantages. I will never wish for what men call the prizes of life. I will ever, with Thy grace, make much of those who are despised or neglected, honor the poor, revere the suffering, and admire and venerate Thy saints and confessors, and take my part with them in spite of the world.

And lastly, O my dear Lord, though I am so very weak that I am not fit to ask Thee for suffering as a gift, and have not strength to do so, at least I will beg of Thee grace to meet suffering well, when Thou in Thy love and wisdom dost bring it upon me. Let me bear pain, reproach, disappointment, slander, anxiety, suspense, as Thou wouldest have me, O my Jesu, and as Thou by Thine own suffering hast taught me, when it comes. And I promise too, with Thy grace, that I will never set myself up, never seek pre-eminence, never court any great thing of the world, never prefer myself to others. I wish to bear insult meekly, and to return good for evil. I wish to humble myself in all things, and to be silent when I am ill-used, and to be patient when sorrow or pain is prolonged, and all for the love of Thee, and Thy Cross, knowing that in this way I shall gain the promise both of this life and of the next.

TEMPLES OF THE HOLY SPIRIT

I adore Thee, O Eternal Word, for Thy gracious condescension, in not only taking a created nature, a created spirit or soul, but a material body. The Most High decreed that for ever and ever He would subject Himself to a created prison. He who from eternity was nothing but infinite incomprehensible Spirit, beyond all laws but those of His own transcendent Greatness, willed that for the eternity to come He should be united, in the most intimate of unions, with that which was under the conditions of a creature. Thy omnipotence, O Lord, ever protects itself — but nothing short of that omnipotence could enable Thee so to condescend without a loss of power. Thy Body has part in Thy power, rather than Thou hast part in its weakness. For this reason, my God, it was that Thou couldst not but rise again, if Thou wast to die — because Thy Body, once taken by Thee, never was or could be separated from Thee, even in the grave. It was Thy Body even then, it could see no corruption; it could not remain under the power of death, for Thou hadst already wonderfully made it Thine, and whatever was Thine must last in its perfection forever. I adore Thy Most Holy Body, O My dear Jesus, the instrument of our redemption!

I look at Thee, my Lord Jesus, and think of Thy Most Holy Body, and I keep it before me as the pledge of my own resurrection. Though I die, as die I certainly shall, nevertheless I shall not forever die, for I shall rise again. My Lord, the heathen who knew Thee not thought the body to be of a miserable and contemptible nature — they thought it the seat, the cause, the excuse of all moral evil. When their thoughts soared highest, and they thought of a future life, they considered that the destruction of the body was the condition of that higher existence. That the body was really part of themselves, and that its restoration could be a privilege, was beyond their utmost imagination. And indeed, what mind of man, O Lord, could ever have fancied without Thy revelation that what, according to our experience, is so vile, so degraded, so animal, so sinful, which is our fellowship with the brutes, which is full of corruption and becomes dust and ashes, was in its very nature capable of so high a destiny, that it could become celestial and immortal without ceasing to be a body! And who but Thou, who art omnipotent, could have made it so? No wonder then, that the wise men of the world, who did not believe in Thee, scoffed at the Resurrection. But I, by Thy grace, will ever keep before me how differently I have been taught by Thee. O best and first and truest of Teachers! O Thou who art the Truth, I know and believe with my whole heart, that this very flesh of mine will rise again. I know, base and odious as it is at present, that it will one day, if I be worthy, be raised incorruptible and altogether beautiful and glorious. This I know; this, by Thy grace, I will ever keep before me.

O my God, teach me so to live, as one who does believe the great dignity, the great sanctity of that material frame in which Thou hast lodged me. And therefore, O my dear Savior, do I come so often and so earnestly to be partaker of Thy Body and Blood, that by means of Thine own ineffable holiness I may be made holy. O my Lord Jesu, I know what is written, that our bodies are the temples of the Holy Spirit. Should I not venerate that which Thou dost miraculously feed, and which Thy Co-equal Spirit inhabits? O my God, who wast nailed to the Cross, "pierce Thou my flesh with Thy fear"; crucify my soul and body and all that is sinful in them, and make me pure as Thou art pure.

GOD ALONE

Thomas says to Him, "My Lord and My God."

I adore Thee, O my God, with Thomas; and if I have, like him, sinned through unbelief, I adore Thee the more. I adore Thee as the One Adorable, I adore Thee as more glorious in Thy humiliation, when men despised Thee, than when Angels worshipped Thee. "My God and my all!" To have Thee is to have everything I can have. O my Eternal Father, give me Thyself. I dared not have made so bold a request, it would have been presumption, unless Thou hadst encouraged me. Thou hast put it into my mouth, Thou hast clothed Thyself in my nature, Thou hast become my Brother, Thou hast died as other men die, only in far greater bitterness, so that, instead of my eyeing Thee fearfully from afar, I might confidently draw near to Thee. Thou dost speak to me as Thou didst speak to Thomas, and dost beckon me to take hold of Thee. My God and my all, what could I say more than this, if I spoke to all eternity? I am full and abound and overflow when I have Thee; but without Thee I am nothing — I wither away, I dissolve and perish. My Lord and my God, my God and my all: give me Thyself and nothing else.

Thomas came and touched Thy sacred wounds. O will the day ever come when I shall be allowed actually and visibly to kiss them? What a day will that be when I am thoroughly cleansed from all impurity and sin, and am fit to draw near to my Incarnate God in His palace of light above! What a morning, when having done with all suffering, I see Thee for the first time with these very eyes of mine, see Thy countenance, gaze upon Thine eyes and gracious lips without quailing and then kneel down with joy to kiss Thy feet, and am welcomed into Thine arms! O my only true Lover, the only Lover of my soul, Thee will I love now, that I may love Thee then. What a day, a long day without ending, the day of eternity, when I shall be so unlike what I am *now*, when I feel in myself a body of death, and am perplexed and distracted with ten thousand thoughts, any one of which would keep me from heaven. O my Lord, what a day when I shall have done once for all with all sins, venial as well as mortal, and shall stand perfect and acceptable in Thy sight, able to bear Thy presence, nothing shrinking from Thine eye, not shrinking from the pure scrutiny of Angels and Archangels, when I stand in the midst and they around me!

O my God, though I am not fit to see or touch Thee yet, still I will ever come within Thy reach, and desire that which is not yet given me in its fullness. O my Savior, Thou shalt be my sole God! I will have no Lord but Thee! I will break to pieces all idols in my heart which rival Thee. I will have nothing but Jesus and Him crucified. It shall be my life to pray to Thee, to offer myself to Thee, to keep Thee before me, to worship Thee in Thy holy sacrifice, and to surrender myself to Thee in Holy Communion.

THE FORBEARANCE OF JESUS

"See My hands and My feet, that it is I Myself; handle Me and see; for a spirit has not flesh and bones as you see that I have." And while they still disbelieved for joy, and wondered, He said to them, "Have you anything here to eat?" Luke 24:39-41.

I adore Thee, O my Lord, for Thy wonderful patience and Thy compassionate tender-hearted condescension. Thy disciples, in spite of all Thy teaching and miracles, disbelieved Thee when they saw Thee die, and fled. Nor did they take courage afterwards, nor think of Thy promise of rising again on the third day. They did not believe Magdalene, nor the other women, who said they had seen Thee alive again. Yet Thou didst appear to them — Thou didst show them Thy wounds — Thou didst let them touch Thee — Thou didst eat before them, and give them Thy peace. O Jesu, is any obstinacy too great for Thy love? Does any number of falls and relapses vanquish the faithfulness and endurance of Thy compassion? Thou dost forgive not only seven times, but to seventy times seven. Many waters cannot quench a love like Thine. And such Thou art over all the earth, even to the end — forgiving, sparing, forbearing, waiting, though sinners are ever provoking Thee; pitying and taking into account their ignorance, visiting all men, all Thine enemies, with the gentle pleadings of Thy grace, day after day, year after year, up to the hour of their death — for He knoweth whereof we are made; He knoweth we are but dust.

My God, what hast Thou done for me! Men say of Thee, O my only Good, that Thy judgments are severe, and Thy punishments excessive. All I can say is that I have not found them so in my own case. Let others speak for themselves, and Thou will meet and overcome them to their own confusion in the day of reckoning. With them I have nothing to do — *Thou* wilt settle with them — but for me the only experience that *I* have is Thy dealings with myself, and here I bear witness, as I know so entirely and feel so intimately, that to me Thou hast been nothing but forbearance and mercy. O how Thou dost forget that I have ever rebelled against Thee! Again and again dost Thou help me. I fall, yet Thou dost not cast me off. In spite of all my sins, Thou dost still love me, prosper me, comfort me, surround me with blessings, sustain me, and further me. I grieve Thy good grace, yet Thou dost give me more. I insult Thee, yet Thou never dost take offence, but art as kind as if I had nothing to explain, to repent of, to amend — as if I were Thy best, most faithful, most steady and loyal friend. Nay, alas! I am even led to presume upon Thy love, it is so like easiness and indulgence, though I ought to fear Thee. I confess it, O my true Savior, every day is but a fresh memorial of Thine unwearied, unconquerable love!

O my God, endure me still — bear with me in spite of my waywardness, perverseness, and ingratitude! I improve very slowly, but really I am moving on to heaven, or at least I wish to move. I am putting Thee before me, unworthy sinner as I am, and I am really thinking in earnest of saving my soul. Give me time to collect my thoughts, and make one good effort. I protest I will put off this languor and lukewarmness — I will shake myself from this sullenness and despondency and gloom — I will rouse myself, and be cheerful, and walk in Thy light. I will have no hope or joy but Thee. Only give me Thy grace — meet me with Thy grace, I will through Thy grace do what I can — and Thou shalt perfect it for me. Then I shall have happy days in Thy presence, and in the sight and adoration of Thy five Sacred Wounds.

THE FAMILIARITY OF JESUS

The Holy Baptist was separated from the world. He was a Nazarite. He went out from the world, and placed himself over against it, and spoke to it from his vantage ground, and called it to repentance. Then went out all Jerusalem to him into the desert, and he confronted them face to face. But in his teaching he spoke of One who should come to them and speak to them in a far different way. He should not separate Himself from them, He should not display Himself as some higher being, but as their Brother, as of their flesh and of their bones, as one among many brethren, as one of the multitude and amidst them. Nay, He was among them already. "There hath stood in the midst of you one whom you know not." That greater one called Himself the Son of man — He was content to be taken as ordinary in all respects, though He was the Highest. St. John and the other Evangelists, though so different in the character of their accounts of Him, agree most strikingly here. The Baptist says, "There is in the midst of you One whom you know not." Next we read of his pointing Jesus out privately, not to crowds, but to one or two of his own religious followers; then of their seeking Jesus and being allowed to follow Him home. At length Jesus begins to disclose Himself and to manifest His glory in miracles; but where? At a marriage feast, where there was often excess, as the master of the feast implies. And how does he manifest his glory? In adding to the wine, the instrument of such excess when it occurred. He was at that marriage feast not as a teacher, but as a guest, and (so to speak) in a social way, for He was with His Mother. Now compare this with what He says in St. Matthew's Gospel of Himself: "John came neither eating nor drinking; the Son of man came eating and drinking, and they say, Behold a man who is a glutton and wine-bibber." John might be hated, but he was respected. Jesus was despised. In Mark we read: "And they were astonished at His teaching, for He taught them as one who had authority, and not as the scribes. . . .And they were all amazed, so that they questioned among themselves, saying, 'What is this? A new teaching!'. . . . And when his friends heard it, they went out to seize him, for they said, 'He is beside Himself.' " (Mark 1:22, 27, 37 and 3:21). This shows the astonishment and rudeness of all about Him. The objection occurs *at once*. Mark 2:16: "And the scribes of the Pharisees, when they saw that *he was eating with sinners and tax collectors*, said to his disciples, 'Why does he eat with tax collectors and sinners?'" What a marked feature it must have been of our Lord's character and mission, since two Evangelists, so independent in their narrations, record it! The prophet had said the same: "He shall grow up before Him as a tender plant, and as a root out of a dry ground: He hath no form nor comeliness, and when we shall see Him, there is no beauty that we should desire Him." (Isa. 53)

This was, O dear Lord, because Thou so lovest this human nature which Thou hast created. Thou didst not love us merely as Thy creatures, the work of Thy hands, but as men. Thou lovest all, for Thou hast created all; but Thou lovest human kind more than all. How is it, Lord, that this should be? What is there in us above others? *Quid est homo, quod memor es ejus?* yet, *nusquam Angelos apprehendit* —"What is man that Thou art mindful of him? . . . ."Nowhere doth he take hold of the angels." Who can sound the depth of Thy counsels and decrees? Thou hast loved man more than Thou hast loved the Angels; and therefore, as Thou didst not take on Thee an angelic nature when Thou didst manifest Thyself for our salvation, so too Thou wouldest not come in any shape or capacity or office which was above the course of ordinary human life — not as a Nazarite, not as a Levitical priest, not as a monk, not as a hermit — but in the fullness and exactness of that human nature which Thou lovest so much. Thou camest not only as a perfect man, but as proper man [a distinct individual]; not formed anew out of earth, not with the spiritual body which Thou now hast, but in that very flesh which had fallen in Adam, and with all our infirmities, all our feelings and sympathies, sin excepted.

O Jesu, it became Thee, the great God, thus abundantly and largely to do Thy work for which the Father sent Thee. Thou didst not do it by halves — and, while that magnificence of sacrifice is Thy glory as God, it is our consolation and aid as sinners. O dearest Lord, Thou art more fully man than the holy Baptist, than St. John, Apostle and Evangelist, than Thine own sweet Mother. As in divine knowledge of me Thou art beyond them all, so also in experience and personal knowledge of my nature. Thou art my elder Brother. How can I fear, how could I not repose my whole heart on one so gentle, so tender, so familiar, so unpretending, so modest, so natural, so humble? Thou art now, though in heaven, just the same as Thou wast on earth: the mighty God, yet the little child — the all-holy, yet the all-sensitive, all-human.

JESUS THE HIDDEN GOD

Be not faithless, but believing. John 20:27b.

I adore Thee, O my God, who art so awful, because Thou art hidden and unseen! I adore Thee, and I desire to live by faith in what I do not see; and considering what I am, a disinherited outcast, I think it has indeed gone well with me that I am allowed, O my unseen Lord and Savior, to worship Thee anyhow. O my God, I know that it is sin that has separated me from Thee. I know that it is sin that has brought on me the penalty of ignorance. Adam, before he fell, was visited by

Angels. Thy saints, too, who keep close to Thee, see visions and in many ways are brought into sensible perception of Thy presence. But to a sinner such as I am, what is left but to possess Thee without seeing Thee? Ah! should I not rejoice at having that most extreme mercy and favor of possessing Thee at all? It is sin that has reduced me to live by faith, as I must at best, and should I not rejoice in such a life, O Lord my God? I see and know, O my good Jesus, that the only way in which I can possibly approach Thee in this world is the way of faith, faith in what Thou hast told me, and I thankfully follow this only way which Thou hast given me.

O my God, Thou dost over-abound in mercy! To live by faith is my necessity, from my present state of being and from my sin; but Thou hast pronounced a blessing on it. Thou hast said that I am more blessed if I believe on Thee, than if I saw Thee. Give me to share that blessedness, give it to me in its fullness. Enable me to believe as if I saw; let me have Thee always before me as if Thou were always bodily and sensibly present. Let me ever hold communion with Thee, my hidden, but my living God! Thou art in my innermost heart. Thou art the life of my life. Every breath I breathe, every thought of my mind, every good desire of my heart, is from the presence within me of the unseen God. By nature and by grace Thou art in me. I see Thee not in the material world except dimly, but I recognize Thy voice in my own intimate consciousness. I turn round and say Rabboni! O be ever thus with me; and if I am tempted to leave *Thee*, do not Thou, O my God, leave *me!*

O my dear Savior, would that I had any right to ask to be allowed to make reparation to Thee for all the unbelief of the world, and all the insults offered to Thy name, Thy Word, Thy church, and the sacrament of Thy love! But, alas, I have a long score of unbelief and ingratitude of my own to atone for. Thou art in the Eucharist, verily and indeed; and the world not only disbelieves, but mocks at this gracious truth. Thou didst warn us long ago by Thyself and by Thy Apostles that Thou wouldest hide Thyself from the world. The prophecy is fulfilled more than ever now; but *I* know what the world knows not. O accept my homage, my praise, my adoration! Let me at least not be found wanting. I cannot help the sins of others — but one at least of those whom Thou hast redeemed shall turn round and with a loud voice glorify God. The more men scoff, the more will I believe in Thee, the good God, the good Jesus, the hidden Lord of life, who hast done me nothing else but good from the very first moment that I began to live.

JESUS THE LIGHT OF THE SOUL

I adore Thee, O my God, as the true and only Light! From eternity to eternity, before any creature was, when Thou wast alone, alone but not solitary, for Thou hast ever been Three in One, Thou wast the infinite Light. There was none to see but Thyself. The Father saw that Light in the Son, and the Son in the Father. Such as Thou wast in the beginning, such Thou art now: most separate from all creatures in this Thy uncreated brightness, most glorious, most beautiful. Thy attributes are so many separate and resplendent colors, each as perfect in its own purity and grace as if it were the sole and highest perfection. Nothing created is more than the very shadow of Thee. Bright as are the Angels, they are poor and most unworthy shadows of Thee. They pale and look dim and gather blackness before Thee. They are so feeble beside Thee, that they are unable to gaze upon Thee. The highest Seraphim veil their eyes by deed as well as by work proclaiming Thine unutterable glory. For me, I cannot even look upon the sun, and what is this but a base material emblem of Thee? How should I endure to look even on an Angel? And how could I look upon Thee and live? If I were placed in the illumination of Thy countenance, I should shrivel up like the grass. O most gracious God, who shall approach Thee, being so glorious — yet how can I keep from Thee?

How can I keep from Thee? For Thou, who art the Light of Angels, art the only Light of my soul. Thou enlightenest every man that cometh into this world. I am utterly dark, as dark as hell, without Thee. I droop and shrink when Thou art away. I revive only in proportion as Thou dawnest upon me. Thou comest and goest at Thy will. O my God, I cannot keep Thee! I can only beg of Thee to stay. *Abide with us, Lord, for it is evening.* Remain till morning, and then go not without giving me a blessing. Remain with me till death in this dark valley, when the darkness will end. Remain, O Light of my soul, *for it is evening.* The gloom, which is not Thine, falls over me. I am nothing. I have little command of myself. I cannot do what I would. I am disconsolate and sad. I want something, I know not what. It is Thou that I want, though I so little understand this. I say it and take it on faith; I partially understand it, but very poorly. Shine on me, "O Fire ever burning and never failing"! And I shall begin to see Light, in and through Thy Light, and I shall begin to recognize Thee truly as the Source of Light. *Abide with us.* Stay, sweet Jesus, stay forever. In this decay of nature, give more grace.

Stay with me, and then I shall begin to shine as Thou shinest: so to shine as to be a light to others. The light, O Jesus, will be all from Thee. None of it will be mine. No merit to me. It will be Thou who shinest through me upon others. O let me thus praise Thee, in the way which Thou dost love best, by shining on all those around me. Give light to them as well as to me; light them with me, through me. Teach me to show forth Thy praise, Thy truth, Thy will. Make me preach Thee without preaching — not by words, but by my example and by the catching force, the sympathetic influence, of what I do — by my visible resemblance to Thy saints, and the evident fullness of the love which my heart bears to Thee.

HE ASCENDED

My Lord, I follow Thee up to heaven; as Thou goest up, my heart and mind go with Thee. Never was triumph like this. Thou didst appear a Babe in human flesh at Bethlehem. That flesh, taken from the Blessed Virgin, did not exist before Thou didst form it into a body; it was a new work of Thy hands. And Thy soul was new altogether, created by Thy omnipotence at the moment when Thou didst enter into her sacred breast. That pure soul and body, taken as a garment for Thyself, began on earth and never had been elsewhere. This is the triumph. Earth rises to heaven. I see Thee going up. I see that Form which hung upon the Cross, those scarred hands and feet, that pierced side; they are mounting up to heaven. And the Angels are full of jubilee; the myriads of blessed spirits, which people the glorious expanse, part like the waters to let Thee pass. And the living pavement of God's palaces is cleft in twain, and the Cherubim with flaming swords, who form the rampart of heaven against fallen man, give way and open out, that Thou mayest enter, and Thy saints after Thee. O memorable day!

O memorable day! The Apostles feel it to be so, now that it is come, though they felt so differently before it came. When it was coming they dreaded it. They could not think but it would be a great bereavement; but now, as we read, they returned to Jerusalem "with great joy." O what a time of triumph! They understood it now. They understood how weak it had been in them to grudge their Lord and Master, the glorious Captain of their salvation, the Champion and First-fruits of the human family, this crown of His great work. It was the triumph of redeemed man. It is the completion of his redemption. It was the last act, making the whole sure, for now man is actually in heaven. He has entered into possession of his inheritance. The sinful race has now one of its own children there, its own flesh and blood, in the person of the Eternal Son. O what a wonderful marriage between heaven and earth! It began in sorrow; but now the long travail of that mysterious wedding day is over; the marriage feast is begun; marriage and birth have gone together; man is new-born when Emmanuel enters heaven.

O Emmanuel, O God in our flesh! We too hope, by Thy grace, to follow Thee. We will cling to the skirts of Thy garments, as Thou goest up; for without Thee we cannot ascend. O Emmanuel, what a day of joy when we shall enter heaven! O inexpressible ecstasy, after all trouble! There is none strong but Thee. "Thou dost hold my right hand; Thou dost guide me with Thy counsel, and afterward Thou wilt receive me to glory. For whom have I in heaven but Thee? And there is nothing upon earth that I desire besides Thee. My flesh and my heart may fail, but God is the strength of my heart, and my portion forever." (Psalm 73:23b-26).

HE ASCENDED INTO HEAVEN

My Lord is gone up into Heaven. I adore Thee, Son of Mary, Jesu, Emmanuel, my God and my Savior. I am allowed to adore Thee, my Savior and my own Brother, for Thou art God. I follow Thee in my thoughts, O Thou First-fruits of our race, as I hope one day by Thy grace to follow Thee in my person. To go to heaven is to go to God. God is there and God alone: for perfect bliss is there and nothing else, and none can be blessed who is not bathed and hidden and absorbed in the glory of the Divine Nature. All holy creatures are but the vestment of the Highest, which He has put on forever, and which is bright with His uncreated light. There are many things on earth, and each is its own center, but one Name alone is named above. It is God alone. This is that true supernatural life; and if I would live a supernatural life on earth, and attain to the supernatural eternal life which is in heaven, I have one thing to do, *viz.*, to live on the thought of God here. Teach me this, O God; give me Thy supernatural grace to practice it; to have my reason, affections, intentions, aims, all penetrated and possessed by the love of Thee, plunged and drowned in the one Vision of Thee.

There is but one Name and one Thought above; there are many thoughts below. This is the earthly life which leads to death, *viz.*, to follow the numberless objects and aims and toils and amusements which men pursue on earth. Even good that is here below does not lead to heaven; it is spoilt in the handselling; it perishes in the using; it has no stay, no integrity, no consistency. It runs off into evil before it has well ceased, before it has well begun to be good. It is at best vanity, when it is nothing worse. It has in it commonly the seeds of real sin. My God, I acknowledge all this. My Lord Jesu, I confess and know that Thou only art the True, the Beautiful and the Good. Thou alone canst make me bright and glorious, and canst lead me up after Thee. Thou art the Way, the Truth and the Life, and none but Thee. Earth will never lead me to heaven. Thou alone art the Way. Thou alone.

My God, shall I for one moment doubt where my path lies? Shall I not at once take Thee for my portion? To whom should I go? Thou hast the words of eternal Life. Thou camest down for the very purpose of doing that which no one here below could do for me. None but He who is in Heaven can bring me to Heaven. What strength have I to scale the high mountain? Though I served the world ever so well, though I did my duty in it (as men speak), what could the world do for me, however hard it tried? Though I filled my station well, did good to my fellows, had a fair name or a wide reputation, though I did great deeds and was celebrated, though I had the praise of history, how would all this bring me to Heaven? I choose Thee then for my One Portion, because Thou livest and diest not.

I cast away all idols. I give myself to *Thee*. I pray Thee to teach me, guide me, enable me, and receive me to Thee.

OUR ADVOCATE ABOVE

I adore Thee, O my Lord, as is most fitting, for Thou art gone to heaven to take my part there, and defend my interests. I have One to plead for me with the Lord of all. On earth we try to put ourselves under the protection of powerful men when we have any important business on hand; we know the value of their influence, and we make much of any promise they make us. Thou art omnipotent, and Thou dost exert Thy omnipotence for me. There are millions of men in the world; Thou didst die for them all; but Thou livest for Thy people whom Thou hast chosen out of the world. And still more marvelously dost Thou live for Thy predestinate. Thou hast engraven them upon the palms of Thy hands; their names are ever before Thee. Thou countest the full roll of them; Thou knowest them by heart; Thou dost order the crown of the world for them; and when their number shall be completed, the world shall end.

For me, Thou hast chosen me for present grace — and thus Thou hast put me in the way for future glory. I know perfectly well that, whatever be Thy secret counsels about me, it will be simply, entirely, most really my own fault if I am not written in Thy book. I cannot understand Thee. I cannot understand myself enough to know and be sure of this. Thou hast put me on such especial vantage ground that the prize is almost in my hand. If I am at present in the society of Angels or Saints, it is hard if I cannot make interest with them that the fellowship begun between them and me should endure. Men of the world know how to turn such opportunities to account in their own matters. If Thou hast given me the gift of entreaty, may I not thereby secure that perseverance to the end, which I cannot merit, and which is the sign and assurance of my predestination? I have in my hands all the means of that which I do not yet have, and may infallibly obtain, even though I cannot certainly secure it.

O my Lord, I sink down almost in despair, in utter remorse certainly and disgust at myself, that I so utterly neglect the means which Thou hast put into my hands, content to let things take their course as if grace would infallibly lead to glory without my own trouble in the matter. What shall I say to Thee, O my Savior, except that I am in the chains of habit, feeble, helpless, stunted, growthless, and as if I were meant to walk through life as the inferior creatures do, with my face down to the earth, on my hands and feet, or crawling on, instead of having an erect posture and a heavenward face? O give me what I need — contrition for all those infinitely numerous venial sins, negligences, slovenliness which are the surest foreboding that I am not of Thy predestinate. Who can save me from myself but Thee?

JESUS, OUR ADVOCATE

I cannot penetrate Thy secret decrees, O Lord! I know Thou didst die for all men really; but since Thou hast not effectually willed the salvation of all, and since Thou mightest have done so, it is certain that Thou doest for one what Thou dost not do for another. I cannot tell what has been Thy everlasting purpose about myself, but if I go by all the signs which Thou hast lavished upon me, I may hope that I am one of those whose names are written in Thy Book. But this I know and feel most entirely, what I believe in the case of all men, but know and feel in my own case, that if I do not attain to that crown which I see and which is within my reach, it is entirely my own fault. Thou hast surrounded me from childhood with Thy mercies; Thou hast taken as much pains with me as if I was of importance to Thee, and my loss of Heaven would be Thy loss of me. Thou hast led me on by ten thousand merciful providences; Thou hast brought me near to Thee in the most intimate of ways; Thou hast brought me into Thy house and chamber; Thou hast fed me with Thyself. Dost Thou not love me, really, truly, substantially, efficaciously love me, without any limitation of the word? I know it. I have an utter conviction of it. Thou art ever waiting to do me benefits, to pour upon me blessings. Thou art ever waiting for me to ask Thee to be merciful to me.

Yes, my Lord, Thou dost desire that I should ask Thee; Thou art ever listening for my voice. There is nothing I cannot get from Thee. Oh I confess my heinous neglect of this great privilege. I am very guilty. I have trifled with the highest of gifts, the power to move Omnipotence. How slack I am in praying to Thee for my own needs! How little have I thought of the needs of others! How little have I brought before Thee the needs of the world — of Thy Church! How little have I asked for graces in detail! And for aid in daily needs! How little have I interceded for individuals! How little have I accompanied actions and undertakings, in themselves good, with prayer for Thy guidance and blessing!

O my Lord Jesu, I will use the time. It will be too late to pray when this life is over. There will be no prayer in the grave. Low as I am in all holy sight, I am strong in Thee, and thus I can do much for the Church, for the world, for all I love. O let not the blood of souls be on my head! O let me not walk my own way without thinking of Thee. Let me bring everything before Thee, asking Thy permission for everything I purpose, Thy blessing on everything I do. I will not move without Thee. I will ever lift up my heart to Thee. I will never forget that Thou art my Advocate at the Throne of the Highest. As the dial speaks of the sun, so will I be ruled by Thee above, if Thou wilt take me and rule me. Be it so, my Lord Jesus: I give myself wholly to Thee.

THE PARACLETE, THE LIFE OF ALL THINGS

I adore Thee, my Lord and God, the Eternal Paraclete, co-equal with the Father and Son. I adore Thee as the Life of all that live. Through Thee the whole material universe hangs together and consists, remains in its place, and moves internally in the order and reciprocity of its several parts. Through Thee the earth was brought into its present state, and was matured through its six days to be a habitation for man. Through Thee all trees, herbs and fruits thrive and are perfected. Through Thee the spring comes after winter and renews all things. That wonderful and beautiful, that irresistible burst into life again, in spite of all obstacles, that awful triumph of nature, is but Thy glorious Presence. Through Thee the many tribes of brute animals live day by day, drawing their breath from Thee. Thou art the life of the whole creation, O Eternal Paraclete — and if of this animal and material framework, how much more of the world of spirits! Through Thee, Almighty Lord, the Angels and Saints sing praises in Heaven. Through Thee our own dead souls are quickened to serve Thee. From Thee is every good thought and desire, every good purpose, every good effort, every good success. It is by Thee that sinners are turned into saints. It is by Thee the Church is refreshed and strengthened, and champions start forth, and martyrs are carried on to their crown. Through Thee new relgious orders, new devotions in the Church come into being; new countries are added to the faith, new manifestations and illustrations are given of the ancient Apostolic creed. I praise and adore Thee, my Sovereign, Lord God, the Holy Spirit.

I adore Thee, O dread Lord, for what Thou hast done for my soul. I acknowledge and feel, not only as a matter of faith but of experience, that I cannot have one good thought or do one good act without Thee. I know that if I attempt anything good in my own strength, I shall to a certainty fail. I have bitter experience of this. My God, I am only safe when Thou dost breathe upon me. I am as weak as water, I am utterly impotent without Thee. The minute Thou dost cease to act in me, I begin to languish, to gasp and to faint away. Of my good desires, whatever they may be, of my good aims, aspirations, attempts, successes, habits, practices, Thou art the sole cause and present continual Source. I have nothing but what I have received, and I protest now in Thy presence, O Sovereign Paraclete, that I have nothing to glory in, and everything to be humbled at.

O my dear Lord, how merciful Thou hast been to me. When I was young, Thou didst put into my heart a special devotion to Thee. Thou hast taken me up in my youth, and in my old age Thou wilt not forsake me. Not for my merit, but from Thy free and bountiful love Thou didst put good resolutions into me when I was young, and didst turn me to Thee. Thou wilt never forsake me. I do earnestly trust so — never certainly without fearful provocation on my part. Yet I trust and pray that Thou wilt keep me from that provocation. O keep me from the provocation of lukewarmness and sloth. O my dear Lord, lead me forward from strength to strength, gently, sweetly, tenderly, lovingly, powerfully, effectually, remembering my fretfulness and feebleness, till Thou bringest me into Thy Heaven.

THE PARACLETE, THE LIFE
OF THE CHURCH

I adore Thee, O my Lord, the Third Person of the All-Blessed Trinity, that Thou hast set up in this world of sin a great light upon a hill. Thou hast founded the Church, Thou hast established and maintained it. Thou fillest it continually with Thy gifts, that men may see, and draw near, and take, and live. Thou hast in this way brought down heaven upon earth. For Thou hast set up a great company which Angels visit by that ladder which the Patriarch saw in a vision. Thou hast by Thy Presence restored communion between God above and man below. Thou hast given him that light of grace which is one with and the commencement of the light of glory. I adore and praise Thee for Thine infinite mercy towards us, O my Lord and God.

I adore Thee, O Almighty Lord, the Paraclete, because Thou in Thine infinite compassion hast brought me into Thy Church, the work of Thy supernatural power. I had no claim on Thee for so wonderful a favor over any one else in the whole world. There were many men far better than I by nature, gifted with more pleasing natural gifts, and less stained with sin. Yet Thou, in Thine inscrutable love for me, hast chosen me and brought me into Thy fold. Thou hast a reason for everything Thou doest. I know there must have been an all-wise reason, as we speak in human language, for Thy choosing me and not another — but I know that that reason was something external to myself. I did nothing towards it — I did everything against it. I did everything to thwart Thy purpose. And thus I owe all to Thy grace. I should have lived and died in darkness and sin; I should have become worse and worse the longer I lived; I should have got more to hate and abjure Thee, O Source of my bliss; I should have gotten yearly more fit for hell, and at length I should have gone there, but for Thine incomprehensible love to me. O my God, that overpowering love took me captive. Was any boyhood so impious as some years of mine? Did I not in fact dare Thee to do Thy worst? Ah, how I struggled to get free from Thee; but Thou art stronger than I and Thou hast prevailed! I have not a word to say, but to bow down in awe before the depths of Thy love.

And then, in the course of time, slowly but infallibly didst Thou bring me on in Thy Church. Now then, give me this further grace, Lord, to use all this grace well, and to turn it to my salvation. Teach me, make me to come to the fountains of mercy continually with an awakened, eager mind and with lively devotion. Give me a love of Thy sacraments and ordinances. Teach me to value as I ought, to prize as the inestimable pearl, that pardon which again and again Thou givest me, and the great and heavenly gift of the Presence of Him whose Spirit Thou art, upon the altar. Without Thee I can do nothing, and Thou art there where Thy Church is and Thy sacraments. Give me grace to rest in them forever, till they are lost in the glory of Thy manifestation in the world to come.

THE PARACLETE, THE LIFE OF MY SOUL

My God, I adore Thee for taking on Thee the charge of sinners; of those who not only cannot profit Thee, but who continually grieve and profane Thee. Thou hast taken on Thyself the office of a minister, and that for those who did not ask for it. I adore Thee for Thy incomprehensible condescension in ministering to me. I know and feel, O my God, that Thou mighest have left me, as I wished to be left, to go my own way, to go straight forward in my willfulness and self-trust to hell. Thou mightest have left me in that enmity to Thee which is in itself death. I should at length have died the second death, and should have had no one to blame for it but myself. But Thou, O eternal Father, hast been kinder to me than I am to myself. Thou hast given me, Thou hast poured out upon me Thy grace, and thus I live.

My God, I adore Thee, O eternal Paraclete, the light and life of my soul. Thou mightest have been content with merely giving me good suggestions, inspiring grace and helping from without. Thou mightest thus have led me on, cleansing me with Thy inward virtue when I changed my state from this world to the next. But in Thine infinite compassion Thou hast from the first entered into my soul and taken possession of it. Thou hast made it Thy Temple. Thou dwellest in me by Thy grace in an ineffable way, uniting me to Thyself and the whole company of angels and saints. Nay, as some have held, Thou art present in me, not only by Thy grace, but by Thy eternal substance, as if, though I did not lose my own individuality, yet in some sense I was even here absorbed in God. Nay — as though Thou hadst taken possession of my very body, this earthly, fleshly, wretched tabernacle — even my body is Thy Temple. O astonishing, awful truth! I believe it, I know it, O my God!

O my God, can I sin when Thou art with me so intimately? Can I forget who is with me, who is in me? Can I expel a Divine Inhabitant by that which He abhors more than anything else, which is the one thing in the whole world which is offensive to Him, the only thing which is not His? Would not this be a kind of sin against the Holy Spirit? My God, I have a double security against sinning: first, the dread of such a profanation of all Thou art to me in Thy very Presence; and next, because I do trust that that Presence will preserve me from sin. My God, Thou wilt go from me if

I sin; and I shall be left to my own miserable self. God forbid! I will use what Thou hast given me; I will call on Thee when tried and tempted. I will guard against the sloth and carelessness into which I am continually falling. Through Thee I will never forsake Thee.

THE PARACLETE, THE FOUNT OF LOVE

My God, I adore Thee as the Third Person of the Ever-Blessed Trinity, under the name and designation of Love. Thou art that living love wherewith the Father and the Son love each other. And Thou art the Author of supernatural love in our hearts — "Fount of life, of fire, and of charity." As a fire Thou didst come down from heaven on the day of Pentecost; and as a fire Thou burnest away the dross of sin and vanity in the heart and dost light up the pure flame of devotion and affection. It is Thou who unitest heaven and earth by showing to us the glory and beauty of the Divine Nature, and making us love what is in Itself so winning and transporting. I adore Thee, O uncreated and everlasting Fire, by which our souls live, by which alone they are made fit for Heaven.

My God, the Paraclete, I acknowledge Thee as the Giver of that great gift by which alone we are saved: supernatural love. Man is by nature blind and hard-hearted in all spiritual matters; how is he to reach Heaven? It is by the flame of Thy grace which consumes him in order to new-make him, and so to fit him to enjoy what without Thee he would have no taste for. It is Thou, O Almighty Paraclete, who hast been and art the strength, the vigor and endurance of the martyr in the midst of his torments. Thou art the stay of the confessor in his long, tedious and humiliating toils. Thou art the fire by which the preacher wins souls, without thought of himself in his missionary labors. By Thee we wake up from the death of sin, to exchange the idolatry of the creature for the pure love of the Creator. By Thee we make acts of faith, hope, charity and contrition. By Thee we live in the atmosphere of earth, protected from its infection. By Thee we are able to consecrate ourselves to the sacred ministry and fulfill our awesome responsibilities in it. By the fire which Thou didst kindle within us we pray and meditate and do penance. Our bodies could live if the sun were extinguished as well as our souls could live without Thee.

My most holy Lord and Sanctified, whatever there is of good in me is Thine. Without Thee I should but get worse and worse as years went on, and should tend to be a devil. If I differ at all from the world, it is because Thou hast chosen me out of the world and hast lit up the love of God in my heart. If I differ from Thy saints, it is because I do not ask earnestly enough for Thy grace and for enough of it, and because I do not diligently improve what Thou hast given me. Increase in me this grace of love, in spite of all my unworthiness. It is more precious than anything else in the world. I accept it in place of all the world can give me. O give it to me! It is my life.

GOD ALL-SUFFICIENT

"Show us the Father and we will be satisfied." Jesus said to him, "Have I been with you so long, and yet you do not know me, Philip? He who has seen me has seen the Father." John 14:8-9

The Son is in the Father and the Father in the Son. O adorable mystery which has been from eternity! I adore Thee, O my incomprehensible Creator, before whom I am an atom, a being of yesterday or an hour ago! Go back a few years, and I simply did not exist; I was not in being and things went on without me: but Thou art from eternity; and nothing whatever for one moment could go on without Thee. And from eternity too Thou hast possessed Thy Nature; Thou hast been — this awful glorious mystery — the Son in the Father and the Father in the Son. Whether we be in existence, or whether we be not, Thou art one and the same always, the Son sufficient for the Father and the Father sufficient for the Son — and all other things, in themselves, but vanity. All things once were not, all things might not be, but it would be enough for the Father that He had begotten His co-equal consubstantial Son, and for the Son that He was embraced in the bosom of the eternal Father. O adorable mystery! Human reason has not conducted me to it, but I believe. I believe, because Thou hast spoken, O Lord. I joyfully accept Thy word about Thyself. Thou must know what Thou art — and who else? Not I surely, dust and ashes, except so far as Thou tellest me. I take then Thine own witness, O my Creator! And I believe firmly, I repeat after Thee what I do not understand, because I wish to live a life of faith; and I prefer faith in Thee to trust in myself.

O my great God, from eternity Thou wast sufficient for Thyself! The Father was sufficient for the Son, and the Son for the Father; art Thou not then sufficient for me, a poor creature, Thou so great, I so little! I have a double all-sufficiency in the Father and the Son. I will take then St. Philip's word and say, Show us the Father, and it *suffices* us. It suffices us, for then we are full to overflowing, when we have Thee. O mighty God, strengthen me with Thy strength, console me with Thy everlasting peace, soothe me with the beauty of Thy countenance; enlighten me with Thine uncreated brightness; purify me with the fragrance of Thine ineffable holiness. Bathe me in Thyself, and give me to drink, as far as mortal man may ask, of the rivers of grace which flow from the Father and the Son, the grace of Thy consubstantial, co-eternal Love.

O my God, let me never forget this truth — that not only art Thou my life, but my only Life! Thou art the Way, the Truth, and the Life. Thou art my Life, and the Life of all who live. All people, all I meet, all I see and hear of, live not unless they live by Thee. They live in Thee, or else they live not at all. No one can be saved out of Thee. Let me never forget this in the business of the day. O give me a true love of souls, of those souls for whom Thou didst die. Teach me to pray for their conversion, to do my part towards effecting it. However able they are, however amiable, however high and distinguished, they cannot be saved unless they have Thee. O my all-sufficient Lord, Thou only sufficest! Thy blood is sufficient for the whole world. As Thou art sufficient for me, so Thou art sufficient for the entire race of Adam. O my Lord Jesus, let Thy Cross be more than sufficient for them. Let it be effectual! Let it be effectual for me more than all, lest I "have all and abound," yet bring no fruit to perfection.

GOD ALONE UNCHANGEABLE

"Where I am going you cannot follow me now; but you shall follow afterward." John 13:36b.

Thou alone, O my God, art what Thou ever hast been! Man changes. Thou art unchangeable; nay, even as man Thou hast ever been unchangeable, for Jesus is yesterday and today Himself, and forever. Thy Word endureth in heaven and earth. Thy decrees are fixed; Thy gifts are without repentance. Thy nature, Thy attributes are ever the same. There ever was Father, ever Son, ever Holy Spirit. I adore Thee in the peace and serenity of Thy unchangeableness. I adore Thee in that imperturbable heaven, which is Thyself. Thou wast perfect from the first; nothing couldst Thou gain, and nothing mightest Thou lose. There was nothing that could touch Thee, because there was nothing but what Thou didst create and couldst destroy. Again, I adore Thee in this Thine infinite stability, which is the center and stay of all created things.

Humankind, on the contrary, is ever changing. Not a day passes but I am nearer the grave. Whatever be my age, whatever the number of my years, I am ever narrowing the interval between time and eternity. I am ever changing in myself. Youth is not like age; and I am continually changing, as I pass along out of youth towards the end of life. O my God, I am crumbling away as I go on! I am already dissolving into my first elements. My soul indeed cannot die, for Thou hast made it immortal; but my bodily frame is continually resolving into that dust out of which it was taken. All below heaven changes: spring, summer, autumn, each has its turn. The fortunes of the world change; what was high, lies low; what was low, rises high. Riches take wings and flee away; bereavements happen.

Friends become enemies, and enemies friends. Our wishes, aims, and plans change. There is nothing stable but Thou, O my God! And Thou art the center and life of all who change, who trust Thee as their Father, who look to Thee, and who are content to put themselves into Thy hands.

I know, O my God, I must change if I am to see Thy face! I must undergo the change of death. Body and soul must die to this world. My real self, my soul, must change by a true regeneration. None but the holy can see Thee. Like Peter, I cannot have a blessing now which I shall have afterwards. "Thou canst not follow me now, but thou shalt follow hereafter." O support me, as I proceed in this great, awful happy change, with the grace of Thy unchangeableness. My unchangeableness here below is perseverance in changing. Let me day by day be molded upon Thee, and be changed from glory to glory by ever looking towards Thee, and ever leaning on Thine arm. I know, O Lord, I must go through trial, temptation, and much conflict if I am to come to Thee. I know not what lies before me, but I know as much as this. I know, too, that if Thou art not with me, my change will be for the worse, not for the better. Whatever fortune I have, be I rich or poor, healthy or sick, with friends or without, all will turn to evil if I am not sustained by the Unchangeable. All will turn to good if I have Jesus with me, yesterday and today the same, and forever.

GOD IS LOVE

Jesus saith to him, "Lovest thou Me more than these?" John 21:15

Thou askest us to love Thee, O my God, and Thou art Thyself Love. There was one attribute of Thine which Thou didst exercise from eternity, and that was Love. We hear of no exercise of Thy power whilst Thou wast alone, nor of Thy justice before there were creatures on their trial; nor of Thy wisdom before the acts and works of Thy Providence; but from eternity Thou didst love, for Thou art not only One but Three. The Father loved from eternity His only begotten Son, and the Son returned to Him an equal love. And the Holy Spirit is that Love in substance, wherewith the Father and the Son love one another. This, O Lord, is Thine ineffable and special blessedness. It is love. I adore Thee, O my infinite Love!

And when Thou hadst created us, then Thou didst but love more, if that were possible. Thou didst love not only Thine own Co-equal Self in the multiplied Personality of the Godhead, but Thou didst love Thy creatures also. Thou wast love to us as well as Love in Thyself. Thou wast love to mankind more than to any other creatures. It was love that brought Thee from heaven, and subjected Thee to the laws of a created nature. It was love alone which was able to conquer Thee, the Highest — and bring Thee low. Thou didst die through Thine infinite love of sinners. And it is love which keeps Thee here still, even now that Thou hast ascended on high, under cheap and common outward forms. *O Amor meus*, if Thou wert not infinite Love, wouldst Thou remain here one hour, exposed to slight, indignity and insult? O my God, I do not know what infinity means — but one thing I see, that Thou art loving to a depth and height far beyond any measurement of mine.

And now Thou biddest me love Thee in turn, for Thou hast loved me. Thou wooest me to love Thee specially, above other. Thou dost say, "Lovest thou Me more than these?" O my God, how shameful that such a question need be put to me! Yet, after all, do I really love Thee more than the run of men? The run of men do not really love Thee at all, but put Thee out of their thoughts. They feel it unpleasant to them to think of Thee; they have no sort of heart for Thee, yet Thou hast need to ask me whether I love Thee even a little. Why should I not love Thee much, how can I help loving Thee much, whom Thou hast brought so near to Thyself, whom Thou hast so wonderfully chosen out of the world to be Thine own special servant and son? Have I not cause to love Thee abundantly more than others, though all ought to love Thee? I do not know what Thou hast done for others personally, though Thou hast died for all — but I know what Thou hast done specially for me. Thou hast done that for me, O my love, which ought to make me love Thee with all my powers.

THE SANCTITY OF GOD

Thou art holy, O Lord, in that Thou art infinitely separate from everything but Thyself, and incommunicable. I adore Thee, O Lord, in this Thy proper sanctity and everlasting purity, for that all blessedness comes from within, and nothing touches Thee from without. I adore Thee as infinitely blessed, yet having all Thy blessedness in Thyself. I adore Thee in that perfect and most holy knowledge of Thyself, in which we conceive the generation of the Word. I adore Thee in that infinite and most pure love of Thyself, a love of Thy Son, and Thy Son's love for Thee, in which we conceive the procession of the Holy Spirit. I adore Thee in that blessedness which Thou didst possess in Thyself from all eternity. My God, I do not understand these heavenly things. I use words which I cannot master; but I believe, O God, that to be true which I thus feebly express in human language.

My God, I adore Thee, as holy without, as well as holy within. I adore Thee as holy in all Thy works as well as in Thine own nature. No creature can approach Thy incommunicable sanctity, but Thou dost approach, and touch, and compass, and possess all creatures; and nothing lives but in Thee, and nothing hast Thou created but what is good. I adore Thee as having made everything good after its kind. I adore Thee as having infused Thy preserving and sustaining power into all things while Thou didst create them, so that they continue to live, though Thou dost not touch them, and do not crumble back into nothing. I adore Thee as having put real power into them, so that they are able to act, although from Thee and with Thee and yet of themselves. I adore Thee as having given power to will what is right and Thy holy grace to Thy rational creatures. I adore Thee as having created man upright, and having bountifully given him an integrity of nature, and having filled him with Thy free grace, so that he was like an Angel upon earth. And I adore Thee still more for having given him Thy grace over again in still more copious measure, and with far more lasting fruits, through Thy eternal Son incarnate. In all Thy works Thou art holy, O my God, and I adore Thee in them all.

Holy art Thou in all Thy works, O Lord, and if there is sin in the world it is not from Thee — it is from an enemy, it is from me and mine. To me, to man, be the shame, for we might will what is right and we will what is evil. What a gulf is there between Thee and me, O my Creator — not only as to nature but as to will! Thy will is ever holy; how, O Lord, shall I ever dare approach Thee? What have I to do with Thee? Yet I must approach Thee; Thou wilt call me to Thee when I die, and judge me. Woe is me, for I am a man of unclean lips, and dwell in the midst of a people of unclean lips! Thy Cross, O Lord, shows the distance that is between Thee and me, while it takes that distance away. It shows both my great sinfulness and Thy utter abhorrence of sin. Impart to me, my dear Lord, the doctrine of the Cross in its fullness, that it may not only teach me my alienation from Thee, but convey to me the virtue of Thy reconciliation.

THE KINGDOM OF GOD

O my Lord Jesus, how wonderful were those conversations which Thou didst hold from time to time with Thy disciples after Thy resurrection. When Thou wentest with two of them to Emmaus, Thou didst explain all the prophecies which related to Thyself. And Thou didst commit to the Apostles the Sacraments in fullness, and the truths which it was Thy will to reveal, and the principles and maxims by which Thy Church was to be maintained and governed. And thus Thou didst prepare them for the day of Pentecost (as the risen bodies were put into shape for the Spirit in the Prophet's vision), when life and illumination was to be infused into them. I will think over all Thou didst say to them with a true and simple faith. The "kingdom of God" was Thy sacred subject. Let me never for an instant forget that Thou hast established on earth a kingdom of Thine own, that the Church is Thy work, Thy establishment, Thy instrument; that we are under Thy rule, Thy laws and Thine eye. Let not familiarity with this wonderful truth lead me to be insensible to it — let not the weakness of Thy human representatives lead me to forget that it is Thou who dost speak and act through them. It was just when Thou wast going away, that then Thou didst leave this kingdom of Thine to take Thy place from then on to the end of the world, to speak for Thee, as Thy visible Body, when Thy personal presence, sensible to man, was departing. I will in true loving faith bring Thee before me, teaching all the truths and laws of this kingdom to Thy Apostles, and I will adore Thee while in my thoughts I gaze upon Thee and listen to Thy words.

Come, O my dear Lord, and teach me in like manner. I need it not, and do not ask it, as far as this, that the word of truth which in the beginning was given to the Apostles by Thee, has been handed down from age to age, and has already been taught to me, and Thy Church is the warrant of it. But I need Thee to teach me day by day, according to each day's opportunities and needs. I need Thee to give me that true Divine instinct about revealed matters that, knowing one part, I may be able to anticipate or to approve of others. I need that understanding of the truths about Thyself which may prepare me for all Thy other truths — or at least may save me from conjecturing wrongly about them or commenting falsely upon them. I need the mind of the Spirit, the mind of the holy Fathers, and of the Church by which I may not only say what they say on definite points, but think what they think; in all I need to be saved from an originality of thought, which is not true if it leads away from Thee. Give me the gift of discriminating between true and false in all discourse of mind.

And for that end, give me, O my Lord, that purity of conscience which alone can receive, which alone can improve Thy inspirations. My ears are dull, so that I cannot hear Thy voice. My eyes are dim, so that I cannot see Thy tokens. Thou alone canst quicken my hearing and purge my sight, and cleanse and renew my heart. Teach me, like Mary, to sit at Thy feet, and to hear Thy Word. Give me that true wisdom which seeks Thy will by prayer and meditation, by direct intercourse with Thee more than by reading and reasoning. Give me the discernment to know Thy Voice from the voice of strangers, and to rest upon it and to seek it in the first place, as something external to myself; and answer me through my own mind if I worship and rely on Thee as above and beyond it.

RESIGNATION TO GOD'S WILL

What is it to thee? Follow thou Me. John 21:22b.

O my God, Thou and Thou alone art all-wise and all-knowing! Thou knowest, Thou hast determined everything which will happen to us from first to last.

Thou hast ordered things in the wisest way, and Thou knowest what will be my lot year by year till I die. Thou knowest how long I have to live. Thou knowest how I shall die. Thou hast precisely ordained everything, sin excepted. Every event of my life is the best for me that could be, for it comes from Thee. Thou dost bring me on year by year, by Thy wonderful Providence, from youth to age, with the most perfect wisdom, and with the most perfect love.

My Lord, who camest into this world to do Thy Father's will, not Thine own, give me a most absolute and simple submission to the will of Father and Son. I believe, O my Savior, that Thou knowest just what is best for me. I believe that Thou lovest me better than I love myself, that Thou art all-wise in Thy Providence, and all-powerful in Thy protection. I am as ignorant as Peter was as to what is to happen to me in time to come; but I resign myself entirely to my ignorance, and thank Thee with all my heart that Thou hast taken me out of my own keeping, and instead of putting such a serious charge upon me, hast bidden me put myself into Thy hands. I can ask nothing better than this, to be Thy care, not my own. I protest, O my Lord, that through Thy grace I will follow Thee whithersoever Thou goest, and will not lead the way. I will wait on Thee for Thy guidance, and on obtaining it, I will act upon it in simplicity and without fear. And I promise that I will not be impatient, if at any time I am kept by Thee in darkness and perplexity; nor will I ever complain or fret if I come into any misfortune or anxiety.

I know, O Lord, Thou wilt do Thy part towards me, as I, through Thy grace, desire to do my part towards Thee. I know well Thou never canst forsake those who seek Thee, or canst disappoint those who trust Thee. Yet I know too, the more I pray for Thy protection, the more surely and fully I shall have it. And therefore now I cry out to Thee, and entreat Thee, first that Thou wouldst keep me from myself, and from following any will but Thine. Next I beg of Thee that in Thine infinite compassion Thou wouldest temper Thy will to me, that it may not be severe, but indulgent to me. Visit me not, O my loving Lord —if it be not wrong so to pray — visit me not with those trying visitations which saints alone can bear! Pity my weakness, and lead me heavenwards in a safe and tranquil course. Still I leave all in Thy hands, my dear Savior — I bargain for nothing — only, if Thou shalt bring heavier trials on me, give me more grace — flood me with the fullness of Thy strength and consolation, that they may work in me not death, but life and salvation.

OUR LORD'S PARTING WITH HIS APOSTLES

I adore Thee, O my God, together with Thy apostles, during the forty days in which Thou didst visit them after thy resurrection! So blessed was the time, so calm, so undisturbed from without, that it was good to be there with Thee, and when it was over, they could hardly believe that it was more than begun. How quickly must that first *Tempus Paschale* have flown![1] And they perhaps hardly knew when it was to end. At least, they did not like to anticipate its ending, but were engrossed with the joy of the present moment. O what a

---

[1] *Tempus Paschale* refers to Eastertide, the period from Easter Day to Pentecost in the Church Year.

time of consolation! What a contrast to what had lately taken place! It was their happy time on earth — the foretaste of heaven; not noticed, not interfered with by man. They passed it in wonder, in musing, in adoration, rejoicing in Thy light, O my risen God!

But Thou, O my dear Lord, didst know better than they! They hoped and desired, perhaps fancied, that the resting time, that *refrigerium* — refreshment, would never end till it was superceded by something better. But Thou didst know in Thy eternal wisdom, that in order to arrive at what was higher than any blessing which they were then enjoying, it was fitting, it was necessary, that they should sustain conflict and suffering. Thou knewest well that unless Thou hadst departed, the Paraclete could not have come to them. Therefore Thou didst go that they might gain more by Thy sorrowful absence than by Thy sensible visitations. I adore Thee, O Father, for sending the Son and the Holy Spirit! I adore Thee, O Son, and Thee, O Holy Spirit, for vouchsafing to be sent to us!

O my God, let me never forget that seasons of consolation are refreshments here and nothing more. They are not our abiding state. They will not remain with us, except in heaven. Here they are only intended to prepare us for doing and suffering. I pray Thee, O my God, to give them to me from time to time. Shed over me the sweetness of Thy Presence, lest I faint by the way; lest I find religious service wearisome through my exceeding infirmity, and give over prayer and meditation; lest I go about my daily work in a dry spirit, or am tempted to take pleasure in it for its own sake, and not for Thee. Give me Thy divine consolations from time to time; but let me not rest in them. Let me use them for the purpose for which Thou givest them. Let me not think it grievous, let me not be downcast, if they go. Let them carry me forward in the thought and the desire of heaven.

GOD'S WAYS NOT OUR WAYS

Because I have spoken these things to you, sorrow hath filled your heart. But I tell you the truth: it is expedient for you. John 16:6, 7a.

O my Savior, I adore Thee for Thine infinite wisdom, which sees what we do not see, and orderest all things in its own most perfect way. When Thou didst say to the Apostles that Thou wert going away, they cried out as if Thou hadst, if it may be so said, broken faith with them. They seemed to say to Thee, "O Jesu, did we not leave all things for Thee? Did we not give up home and family, father and wife, friends and neighbors, our habits, our accustomed way of living, that we might join Thee? Did we not divorce ourselves from the world, or rather die to it, that we might be eternally united and live to Thee? And now Thou sayest that Thou art leaving us. Is this reasonable? Is this just? Is this faithfulness to Thy promise? Did we bargain for this? O Lord Jesus, we adore Thee, but we are confounded, and we know not what to say!"

Yet let God be true and every man a liar. Let the Divine Word triumph in our minds over every argument and persuasion of sensible appearances. Let faith rule us and not sight. Thou art justified, O Lord, when Thou art arraigned, and dost gain the cause when Thou art judged. For Thou didst know that the true way of possessing Thee was to lose Thee. Thou didst know that what man stands most of all in need of, and in the first place, is not an outward guide, though he needs that too, but an inward, intimate, invisible aid. Thou didst intend to heal him thoroughly, not slightly; not merely to reform the surface, but to remove and destroy the heart and root of all his ills. Thou then didst purpose to visit his soul, and Thou didst depart in body that Thou mightest come again to him in Spirit. Thou didst not stay with Thine Apostles therefore, as in the days of Thy flesh, but Thou didst come to them and abide with them forever with a much more immediate and true communion in the power of the Paraclete.

O my God, in Thy sight I confess and bewail my extreme weakness, in distrusting, if not Thee, at least Thine own servants and representatives, when things do not turn out as I would have them or as I expected! O my dear Lord, give me a generous faith in Thee and in Thy servants.

GOD THE INCOMMUNICABLE PERFECTION

Almighty God, Thou art the one, infinite Fullness. From eternity Thou art the one and only Absolute and most all-sufficient seat and proper abode of all conceivable best attributes, and of all, which are many more, which cannot be conceived. I hold this as a matter of reason, though my imagination starts from it. I hold it firmly and absolutely, though it is the most difficult of all mysteries. I hold it from the actual experience of Thy blessings and mercies towards me, the evidences of Thy awful Being and attributes, brought home continually to my reason, beyond the power of doubting or disputing. I hold it from that long and intimate familiarity with it, so that it is part of my rational nature to hold it; because I am so constituted and made up upon the idea of it, as a keystone, that not to hold it would be to break my mind to pieces. I hold it from that intimate perception of it in my conscience, as a fact present to me, that I feel it as easy to deny my own personality as the personality of God, and have lost my grounds for believing that I exist myself if I deny existence to Him. I hold it because I could not bear to be without Thee, O my Lord and Life, because I look for blessings beyond thought by being with Thee. I hold it from the terror of being left in this wild world without stay or protection. I hold it from humble love to Thee, from delight in Thy glory and exaltations, from my desire that Thou shouldst be great and the only great One. I hold it for Thy sake, and because I love to think of Thee, as so glorious, perfect and beautiful. There is one God, and none other but He.

Since, O eternal God, Thou art so incommunicably great, so one, so perfect in that oneness, surely one would say, Thou ever must be most distant from Thy creatures if Thou didst create any — separated from them by Thy eternal ancientness on their beginning to be, and separated by Thy transcendency of excellence and Thy absolute contrariety to them. What couldst Thou give them out of Thyself which would suit their nature, so different from Thine? What good of Thine could be their good, or do them good, except in some poor, external way? If Thou couldst be the happiness of man, then might man in turn, or some gift from him, be the happiness of the bird of prey or the wild beast, the cattle of his pasture, or the myriads of minute creatures which we can scarcely see. Mankind is not so far above them as Thou are above it. For what is every creature in Thy sight, O Lord, but a vanity and a breath, a smoke which stays not, but flits by and passes away, a poor thing which only vanishes so much the sooner because Thou lookest on it, and it is set in the illumination of Thy countenance? Is not this, O Lord, the perplexity of reason? From the Perfect comes the Perfect. Yet Thou canst not make a second God, from the nature of the case; and therefore either canst not create at all, or of necessity must create what is infinitely unlike and therefore, in a sense, unworthy of the Creator.

What communion then can there be between Thee and me? O my God! what am I but a parcel of dead bones, a feeble, tottering, miserable being, compared with Thee? I am Thy work, and Thou didst create me pure from sin, but how canst Thou look upon me, in my best estate of nature, with complacency? How canst Thou see in me any image of Thyself, the Creator? How is this, my Lord? Thou didst pronounce Thy work very good, and didst make man in Thine image. Yet there is an infinite gulf between Thee and me, O my God.

GOD COMMUNICATED TO US

Thou hast, O Lord, an incommunicable perfection, but still that Omnipotence by which Thou didst create, is sufficient also to the work of communicating Thyself to the spirits which Thou hast created. Thy almighty Life is not for our destruction, but for our living. Thou remainest ever one and the same in Thyself, but there goes from Thee continually a power and virtue which by its contact is our strength and good. I do not know how this can be; my reason does not satisfy me here; but in nature I see intimations, and by faith I have full assurance of the truth of this mystery. By Thee we cross the gulf that lies between Thee and us. The Living God is lifegiving. Thou art the Fount and Center as well as the Seat of all good. The traces of Thy glory, as the many-colored rays of the sun, are scattered over the whole face of nature, without diminution of Thy perfections, or violations of Thy transcendent and unapproachable Essence. How it can be, I know not; but so it is. And thus, remaining one and sole and infinitely removed from all things, still Thou art the fullness of all things. In Thee they consist, of Thee they partake, and into Thee, retaining their own individuality, they are absorbed. And thus, while we droop and decay in our own nature, we live by Thy breath; and Thy grace enables us to endure Thy presence.

Make me then like Thyself, O my God, since, in spite of myself, such Thou canst make me, such I can be made. Look on me, O my Creator, pity the work of Thy hands, *that I perish not in my infirmity.* Take me out of my natural imbecility, since that is possible for me which is so necessary. Thou hast shown it to be possible in the face of the whole world by the most overwhelming proof, by taking our created nature on Thyself and exalting it in Thee. Give me in my own self the benefit of this wondrous truth, not that it has been so publicly ascertained and guaranteed. Let me have in my own person, what in Jesus Thou hast given to my human nature. Let me be partaker of that divine nature in all the riches of its attributes, which in fullness of substances and in personal presence became the Son of Mary. Give me that life, suitable to my own need, which is stored up for us all in Him who is the Life of men. Teach me and enable me to live the life of saints and angels. Take me out of the languor, the irritability, the sensitiveness, the incapability, the anarchy in which my soul lies, and fill it with Thy fullness. Breath on me, that the dead bones may live. Breathe on me with that Breath which infuses energy and kindles fervor. In asking for fervor, I ask for all that I can need and all that Thou canst give: for it is the crown of all gifts and all virtues. It cannot really and fully be, except where they are all present. It is the beauty and the glory, as it is also the continual safeguard and purifier of them all. In asking for fervor, I am asking for effectual strength, consistency, and perseverance. I am asking for deadness to every human motive, and simplicity of intention to please Thee. I am asking for faith, hope and charity in their most heavenly exercise. In asking for fervor I am asking to be rid of the fear of man and the desire of his praise; I am asking for the gift of prayer, because it will be so sweet; I am asking for that loyal perception of duty which follows on yearning affection. I am asking for sanctity, peace and joy all at once. In asking for fervor I am asking for the brightness of the Cherubim and the fire of the Seraphim, and the whiteness of all saints. In asking for fervor, I am asking for that which, while it implies all gifts, is that in which I signally fail. Nothing would be a trouble to me, nothing a difficulty, if I but had fervor of soul.

Lord, in asking for fervor, I am asking for Thyself, for nothing short of Thee, O my God, who hast given Thyself wholly to us. Enter my heart substantially and personally, and fill it with fervor by filling it with Thee. Thou alone canst fill the soul of man, and Thou hast promised to do so. Thou art the living Flame, and ever burnest with love of man. Enter into me and set me on fire after Thy pattern and likeness.

GOD THE SOLE STAY FOR ETERNITY

My God, I believe and know and adore Thee as infinite in the multiplicity and depth of Thy nature. I adore Thee as containing in Thee an abundance of all that can delight and satisfy the soul. I know, on the contrary, and from sad experience I am too sure, that whatever is created, whatever is earthly pleases but for the time, and then palls and is a weariness. I believe that there is nothing at all here below which I should not get sick of eventually. I believe that, though I had all the means of happiness which this life could give, yet in time I should tire of living, feeling everything trite and dull and unprofitable. I believe, that were it my lot to live the long antediluvian life, and to live it without Thee, I should be utterly, inconceivably wretched at the end of it. I think I should be tempted to destroy myself for very weariness and disgust. I think I should at last lose my reason and go mad if my life here was prolonged long enough. I should feel it like solitary confinement, for I should find myself shut up in myself without companion, if I could not converse with Thee, my God. Thou only, O my infinite Lord, art ever new, though Thou art the ancient of days — the last as well as the first.

Thou, O my God, art ever new, though Thou art the most ancient — Thou alone art the food for eternity. I am to live forever, not for a time — and I have no power over my being; I cannot destroy myself, even though I were so wicked as to wish to do so. I must live on, with intellect and consciousness forever, in spite of myself. Without Thee eternity would be another name for eternal misery. In Thee alone have I that which can stay me up forever. Thou alone art the food of my soul. Thou alone art inexhaustible, and ever offerest to me something new to know, something new to love. At the end of millions of years, I shall know Thee so little that I shall seem to myself only beginnning. At the end of millions of years I shall find in Thee the same, or rather, greater sweetness than at first, and shall seem then only to be beginning to enjoy Thee; and so on for eternity I shall ever be a little child beginning to be taught the rudiments of Thy infinite divine nature. For Thou art Thyself the seat and center of all good, and the only substance in this universe of shadows, and the heaven in which blessed spirits live and rejoice.

My God, I take Thee for my portion. From mere prudence I turn from the world to Thee; I give up the world for Thee. I renounce that which promises, for Him who performs His promises. To whom else should I go? I desire to find and feed on Thee here; I desire to feed of Thee, Jesu, my Lord, who art risen, who hast gone up on high, who yet remainest with Thy people on earth. I look up to Thee. I look for the Living Bread which is in Heaven, which comes down from Heaven. Give me ever of this Bread. Destroy this life which will soon perish — even though Thou dost not destroy it, and fill me with that supernatural Life which will never die.

THE EUCHARIST

I adore Thee, O my Lord God, with the most profound awe for Thy passion and crucifixion in sacrifice for our sins. Thou didst suffer incommunicable sufferings in Thy sinless soul. Thou wast exposed in Thy innocent body to ignominious torments, to mingled pain and shame. Thou wast stripped and fiercely scourged, Thy sacred body vibrating under the heavy flail as trees under the blast. Thou wast, when thus mangled, hung up upon the Cross, naked, a spectacle for all to see Thee quivering and dying. What does all this imply, O mighty God? What a depth is here which we cannot fathom! My God, I know well that Thou couldst have saved us at Thy Word without suffering Thyself. But Thou didst choose to purchase us at the price of Thy Blood. I look on Thee, the Victim lifted up on Calvary, and I know and protest that that death of Thine was an expiation for the sins of the whole world. I believe and know that Thou alone couldst have offered a meritorious atonement; for it was Thy divine Nature which gave Thy sufferings their worth. Rather than that I should perish according to my deserving, Thou wast nailed to the tree and didst die.

Such a sacrifice was not to be forgotten. It was not to be — it could not be — a mere event in the world's history which was to be done and over, and was to pass away except in its obscure, unrecognized effects. If that great deed was what we believe it to be, what we know it is, it must remain present though past; it must be a standing fact for all times. Our own careful reflection on it tells us this; and therefore, when we are told that Thou, O Lord, though Thou hast ascended to glory, hast renewed and perpetuated Thy sacrifice to the end of all things, not only is the news most touching and joyful, as testifying to so tender a Lord and Savior, but it carries with it the full assent and agreement of our reason. Though we neither could, nor would have dared anticipate so wonderful a teaching, yet we adore its very suitableness to Thy perfections as well as its infinite compassionateness for us, now that we are told of it. Yes, my Lord, though Thou hast left the world, Thou art daily offered up in the Mass; and, though Thou canst not suffer pain and death, Thou dost still subject Thyself to indignity and restraint to carry out to the full Thy mercies towards us. Thou dost humble Thyself daily; for, being infinite, Thou couldst not end Thy humiliation while they existed for whom Thou didst submit to it. So Thou remainest a Priest forever.

My Lord, I offer Thee myself in turn as a sacrifice of thanksgiving. Thou hast died for me and I in turn make myself over to Thee. I am not my own. Thou hast bought me; I will by my own act and deed complete the purchase. My wish is to be separated from everything of this world, to cleanse myself wholly from sin, to put away from me even what is innocent if used for its own sake and not for Thine. I put away reputation, honor and influence, and power, for my praise and strength shall be in Thee. Enable me to carry out what I profess.

HOLY COMMUNION

My God, who can be inhabited by Thee except the pure and holy? Sinners may come to Thee, but to whom shouldst Thou come except to the sanctified? My God, I adore Thee as the Holiest; and when Thou didst come upon earth, Thou didst prepare a holy habitation for Thyself in the most chaste womb of the Blessed Virgin. Thou didst make a dwelling place special for Thyself. She did not receive Thee without first being prepared for Thee. From the moment that she was at all, she was filled with Thy grace, and she went on increasing in grace year after year, till the time came when Thou didst send down the Archangel to signify to her Thy presence within her. So holy must be the dwelling place of the Highest. I adore and glorify Thee, O Lord my God, for Thy great holiness.

O my God, holiness becometh Thy House, and yet Thou dost make Thine abode in my breast. My Lord, my Savior, to me Thou comest hidden under the semblance of earthly things, yet in that very flesh and blood which Thou didst take from Mary. Thou who didst first inhabit Mary's breast dost come to me. My God, Thou seest me; I cannot see myself. Were I ever so good a judge about myself, ever so unbiased and with ever so correct a rule of judging, still, from my very nature, I cannot look at myself and view myself truly and wholly. But Thou, as Thou comest to me, contemplatest me. When I say, *Domine, non sum dignus* — "Lord, I am not worthy," Thou whom I am addressing alone understandest in their fullness the words which I use. Thou seest how unworthy so great a sinner is to receive the One Holy God, whom the Seraphim adore with trembling. Thou seest, not only the stains and scars of past sins, but the mutilations, the deep cavities, the chronic disorders which they have left in my soul. Thou seest the innumerable living sins, though they be not mortal, living in their power and presence, their guilt and their penalties, which clothe me. Thou seest all my bad habits, all my mean principles, all wayward, lawless thoughts, my multitudes of infirmities and miseries, yet Thou comest. Thou seest most perfectly how little I really feel what I am now saying, yet Thou comest. O my God, left to myself should I not perish under the awful splendor and the consuming fire of Thy Majesty? Enable me to bear Thee, lest I have to say with Peter, "Depart from me, for I am a sinful man, O Lord!"

My God, enable me to bear Thee, for Thou alone canst. Cleanse my heart and mind from all that is past. Wipe out entirely all my recollections of evil. Rid me of all languor, sickliness, irritability, feebleness of soul. Give me a true perception of things unseen, and make me truly, practically and in the details of life, prefer Thee to anything on earth, and the future world to the present. Give me courage, a true instinct discerning between right and wrong, humility in all things, and a tender, longing love of Thee.

THE FOOD OF THE SOUL

For Thee my soul hath thirsted. Psalm 63:1

In Thee, O Lord, all things live, and Thou dost give them their food. "The eyes of all hope in Thee." To the beast of the field Thou givest meat and drink. They live on day by day, because Thou dost give them day by day to live. And, if Thou givest not, they feel their misery at once. Nature witnesses to this great truth, for they are visited at once with great agony, and they cry out and wildly wander about, seeking what they need. But, as to us Thy children, Thou feedest us with another food. Thou knowest, O my God, who madest us, that nothing can satisfy us but Thyself, and therefore Thou hast caused Thine own Self to be food and drink to us. O most adorable mystery! O most stupendous of mercies! Thou most Glorious, and Beautiful, and Strong and Sweet, Thou didst know well that nothing else would support our immortal natures, our frail hearts, but Thyself. And so Thou didst take human flesh and blood, that they, as being the flesh and blood of God, might be our life.

O what an awful thought! Thou dealest otherwise with others, but, as to me, the flesh and blood of God is my sole life. I shall perish without it; yet shall I not perish with it and by it? How can I raise myself to such an act as to feed upon God? O my God, I am in a strait — shall I go forward, or shall I go back? I will go forward: I will go to meet Thee. I will open my mouth, and receive Thy gift. I do so with great awe and fear, but what else can I do? To whom should I go but to Thee? Who can save me but Thou? Who can cleanse me but Thou? Who can make me overcome myself but Thou? Who can raise my body from the grave but Thou? Therefore I come to Thee in all these my necessities, in fear, but in faith.

My God, Thou art my life; if I leave Thee, I cannot but thirst. Lost spirits thirst in hell, because they have not God. They thirst, though they fain would have it otherwise, from the necessity of their original nature. But I, my God, wish to thirst for Thee with a better thirst. I wish to be clad in that new nature, which so longs for Thee from loving Thee, as to overcome in me the fear of coming to Thee. I come to Thee, O Lord, not only because I am unhappy without Thee, not only because I feel I need Thee, but because Thy grace draws me on to seek Thee for Thine own sake, because Thou art so glorious and beautiful. I come in great fear, but in greater love. O may I never lose, as years pass away and the heart shuts up and all things become a burden, let me never lose this youthful, eager, elastic love of Thee. Make Thy grace supply the failure of nature. Do the more for me, the less I can do for myself. The more I refuse to open my heart to Thee, so much the fuller and stronger be Thy supernatural visitings, and the more urgent and efficacious Thy presence in me.

THE SACRED HEART

O Sacred Heart of Jesus, I adore Thee in the oneness of the personality of the Second Person of the Holy Trinity. Whatever belongs to the Person of Jesus, belongs therefore to God, and is to be worshipped with that one and same worship which we pay to Jesus. He did not take on Him His human nature as something distinct and separate from Himself, but as simply, absolutely, eternally His, so as to be included by us in the very thought of Him. I worship Thee, O Heart of Jesus, as being Jesus Himself, as being that eternal Word in human nature which He took wholly and lives in wholly, and therefore in Thee. Thou art the Heart of the Most High made man. In worshipping Thee, I worship my incarnate God, Emmanuel. I worship Thee as bearing a part in that passion which is my life, for Thou didst burst and break through agony, in the garden of Gethsemane, and Thy precious contents trickled out through the veins and pores of the skin, upon the earth. And again, Thou hadst been drained all but dry upon the Cross; and then, after death, Thou wast pierced by the lance, and gavest out the small remains of that inestimable treasure which is our redemption.

My God, my Savior, I adore Thy Sacred Heart, for that heart is the seat and source of all Thy tenderest human affections for us sinners. It is the instrument and organ of Thy love. It did beat for us. It yearned over us. It ached for us and for our salvation. It was on fire through zeal, that the glory of God might be manifested in and by us. It is the channel through which has come to us all Thy overflowing human affection, all Thy divine charity towards us. All Thine incomprehensible compassion for us, as God and Man, as our Creator and Redeemer and Judge, has come to us, and comes, in one inseparably mingled stream, through that Sacred Heart. O most sacred symbol and sacrament of love, divine and human, in its fullness: Thou didst save me by Thy divine strength and Thy human affection, and then at length, by that wonder-working blood wherewith Thou didst overflow.

O most Sacred, most loving Heart of Jesus: Thou art concealed in the Holy Eucharist, and Thou beatest for us still. Now as then Thou sayest, "With desire I have desired." I worship Thee, then, with all my best love and awe, with my fervent affection, with my most subdued, most resolved will. O my God, when Thou dost condescend to allow me to receive Thee, to eat and drink of Thee, and when Thou for a while takest up Thy abode within me, O make my heart beat with Thy Heart. Purify it of all that is earthly, all that is proud and sensual, all that is hard and cruel, of all perversity, of all disorder, of all deadness. So fill it with Thee, that neither the events of the day nor the circumstances of the time may have power to ruffle it; but that in Thy love and Thy fear it may have peace.

THE INFINITE PERFECTION OF GOD

Of Him and through Him and in Him Are All Things. Rom. 11:36

Of Him. I adore Thee, O my God, as the origin and source of all that is in the world. Once nothing was in being but Thee. It was so for a whole eternity. Thou alone hast had no beginning. Thou hast ever been in being without beginning. Thou hast necessarily been a whole eternity by Thyself, having in Thee all perfections stored up in Thyself, by Thyself; a world of worlds, an infinite abyss of all that is great and wonderful, beautiful and holy; a treasury of infinite attributes, all in one; infinitely one while thus infinitely various. My God, the thought simply exceeds a created nature, much more my own. I cannot attain to it; I can but use the words and say, "I believe," without comprehending. But this I can do: I can adore Thee, O my great and good God, as the one source of all perfection, and that I do, and with Thy grace will do always.

Through Him. And when other beings began to be, they lived through Thee. They did not begin of themselves. They did not come into existence except by Thy determinate will, by Thy eternal counsel, by Thy sole operation. They are wholly from Thee. From eternity, in the deep ocean of Thy blessedness, Thou didst predestinate everything which in its hour took place. Not a substance, ever so insignificant, but is Thy design and Thy work. Much more, not a soul comes into being, but by Thy direct appointment and act. Thou seest, Thou hast seen from all eternity, every individual of Thy creatures. Thou hast seen me, O my God, from all eternity. Thou seest distinctly and ever hast seen, whether I am to be saved or to be lost. Thou seest my history through all ages in heaven or in hell. O awful thought! My God, enable me to bear it, lest the thought of Thee confound me utterly; and lead me forward to salvation.

In Him. And I believe and know, moreover, that all things live in Thee. Whatever there is of being, of life, of excellence, of enjoyment, of happiness, in the whole creation, is, in its substance, simply and absolutely Thine. It is by dipping into the ocean of Thy infinite perfections that all beings have whatever they have of good. All the beautifulness and majesty of the visible world is a shadow or a glimpse of Thee, or the manifestation or operation in a created medium of one or other of Thy attributes. All that is wonderful in the way of talent or genius is but an unworthy reflection of the faintest gleam of the eternal Mind. Whatever we do well is not only by Thy help, but is after all scarcely an imitation of that sanctity which is in fullness in Thee. O my God, shall I one day see Thee? What sight can compare to that great sight! Shall I see the source of that grace which enlightens me, strengthens me, and consoles me? As I came from Thee, as I am made through Thee, as I live in Thee, so, O my God, may I at last return to Thee and be with Thee for ever and ever.

THE INFINITE KNOWLEDGE OF GOD

All things are naked and open to His eyes; neither is there any creature invisible in His sight. Hebrews 4:13

My God, I adore Thee, as beholding all things. Thou knowest in a way altogether different and higher than any knowledge which can belong to creatures. We know by means of sight and thought; there are few things we know in any other way; but how unlike this knowledge, not only in extent, but in its nature and its characteristics, is Thy knowledge! The Angels know many things, but their knowledge compared to Thine is mere ignorance. The human soul, which Thou didst take into Thyself when Thou didst become man, was filled from the first with all the knowledge possible to human nature: but even that was nothing but a drop compared to the abyss of that knowledge and its keen luminousness, which is Thine as God.

My God, could it be otherwise? For from the first and from everlasting Thou wast by Thyself; and Thy blessedness consisted in knowing and contemplating Thyself, the Father in the Son and the Spirit, and the Son and Spirit severally in each other and in the Father, thus infinitely comprehending the infinite. If Thou didst know Thy infinite self thus perfectly, Thou didst know that which was greater and more than anything else could be. All that the whole universe contains, put together, is after all but finite. It is finite, though it be illimitable! It is finite, though it be so multiform; It is finite, though it be so marvelously skillful, beautiful and magnificent; but Thou art the infinite God, and, knowing Thyself, much more dost Thou know the whole universe, however vast, however intricate and various, and all that is in it.

My great God, Thou knowest all that is in the universe, because Thou Thyself didst make it. It is the very work of Thy hands. Thou art Omniscient because Thou art Omni-creative. Thou knowest each part, however minute, as perfectly as Thou knowest the whole. Thou knowest mind as perfectly as Thou knowest matter. Thou knowest the thoughts and purposes of every soul as perfectly as if there were no other soul in the whole of Thy creation. Thou knowest me through and through; all my present, past and future are before Thee as one whole. Thou seest all those delicate and evanescent motions of my thought which altogether escape myself. Thou canst trace every act, whether deed or thought, to its origin, and canst follow it into its whole growth and consequences. Thou knowest how it will be with me at the end; Thou hast before Thee that hour when I shall come to Thee to be judged. How awful is the prospect of finding myself in the presence of my Judge! Yet, O Lord, I would not that Thou shouldst not know me. It is my greatest stay to know that Thou readest my heart. O give me more of that open-hearted sincerity which I have desired. Keep me ever from being afraid of Thine eye, from the inward consciousness that I am not honestly trying to please Thee. Teach me to love Thee more, and then I shall be at peace, without any fear of Thee at all.

THE PROVIDENCE OF GOD

I adore Thee, my God, as having laid down the ends and the means of all things which Thou hast created. Thou hast created everything for some end of its own, and Thou dost direct it to that end. The end, which Thou didst in the beginning appoint for man, is Thy worship and service, and his own happiness in paying it; a blessed eternity of soul and body with Thee forever. Thou hast provided for this, and that in the case of every man. As Thy hand and eye are upon the

brute creation, so are they upon us. Thou sustainest
everything in life and action for its own end. Not a rep-
tile, not an insect, but Thou seest and makest to live,
while its time lasts. Not a sinner, not an idolater, not a
blasphemer, not an atheist lives but by Thee, and in
order that he may repent. Thou art careful and tender
to each of the beings that Thou has created, as if it were
the only one in the world. For Thou canst see every one
of them at once, and Thou lovest every one in this mortal life, and pursuest every one by itself with all the
fullness of Thy attributes, as if Thou wast waiting on it
and ministering to it for its own sake. My God, I love to
contemplate Thee, I love to adore Thee, thus the
wonderful Worker of all things every day in every
place.

All Thy acts of providence are acts of love. If Thou
sendest evil upon us, it is in love. All the evils of the
physical world are intended for the good of Thy
creatures, or are the unavoidable attendants on that
good. And Thou turnest that evil into good. Thou
visitest men with evil to bring them to repentance, to
increase their virtue, to gain for them greater good
hereafter. Nothing is done in vain, but has its gracious
end. Thou dost punish, yet in wrath Thou dost
remember mercy. Even Thy justice when it overtakes
the impenitent sinner who had exhausted Thy loving
providences towards him, is mercy to others, as saving
them from his contaminations or granting them a warn-
ing. I acknowledge with a full and firm faith, O Lord,
the wisdom and goodness of Thy Providence, even in
Thine inscrutible judgments and Thine incomprehensible decrees.

O my God, my whole life has been a course of mercies and blessings shown to one who has been most unworthy of them. I require no faith, for I have had long

experience as to Thy providence towards me. Year after year Thou hast carried me on — removed dangers from my path — recovered me, recruited me, refreshed me, borne with me, directed me, sustained me. O forsake me not when my strength faileth me. And Thou never wilt forsake me. I may securely repose upon Thee, sinner as I am, nevertheless, while I am true to Thee, Thou wilt still, and to the end, be superabundantly true to me. I may rest upon Thine arm; I may go to sleep in Thy bosom. Only give me, and increase in me, that true loyalty to Thee which is the bond of the covenant between Thee and me, and the pledge in my own heart and conscience that Thou, the Supreme God, wilt not forsake me, the most miserable of Thy children.

GOD IS ALL IN ALL

One God and Father of all, who is above all, and through all, and in us all. Ephesians 4:6

God alone is in Heaven. God is all in all. Eternal Lord, I acknowledge this truth, and I adore Thee in this sovereign and most glorious mystery. There is One God, and He fills Heaven; and all blessed creatures, though they ever remain in their individuality, are, as the very means of their blessedness, absorbed, and (as it were) drowned in the fullness of Him who is *super omnes, et per omnia, et in omnibus* — "above all, and through all and in all." If ever, through Thy grace, I attain to see Thee in Heaven, I shall see nothing else but Thee, because I shall see all whom I see in Thee, and seeing them I shall see Thee. As I cannot see things here below without light, and to see them is to see the rays which come from them, so in that Eternal City *claritas Dei illuminavit eam, et lucerna ejus est Agnus* — "the glory of God did lighten it, and the Lamb is the light thereof." (Rev. 21:23). My God, I adore Thee now (at least I will do so to the best of my powers) as the one, sole, true Life and Light of the soul, as I shall know and see Thee to be hereafter, if by Thy grace I attain to Heaven.

Eternal, incomprehensible God, I believe and confess and adore Thee as being infinitely more wonderful, resourceful, and immense than this universe which I see. I look into the depths of space, in which the stars are scattered about, and I understand that I should be millions upon millions of years in creeping along from one end of it to the other, if a bridge were thrown across it. I consider the overpowering variety, richness, intricacy of Thy work; the elements, principles, laws, results which go to make it up. I try to recount the multitude of kinds of knowledge, of sciences, and of arts of which it can be made the subject. And I know, I should be ages upon ages in learning everything that is to be learned about this world, supposing that I had the power of learning it at all. And new sciences would come to light, at present unsuspected, as fast as I had mastered the old, and the conclusions of today would be nothing more than starting points of tomorrow. And I see moreover, and the more I examined it, the more I should understand, the marvelous beauty of these works of Thy hands. And so, I might begin again after this material universe, and find a new world of knowledge, higher and more wonderful in Thy intellectual creations, Thy angels and other spirits, and mankind. But all, all that is in these worlds — high and low — are but an atom compared with the grandeur, the height and depth, the glory on which Thy saints are gazing in their contemplation of Thee. It is the occupation of eternity, ever new, inexhaustible, ineffably ecstatic, the stay and blessedness of existence, thus to drink in and be dissolved in Thee.

My God, it was Thy supreme blessedness in the eternity past, as it is Thy blessedness in all eternities, to know Thyself as Thou alone canst know Thee. It was by seeing Thyself in Thy co-equal Son and Thy co-eternal Spirit and in their seeing Thee, that Father, Son and Holy Spirit, three Persons, one God, was infinitely blessed. O my God, what am I that Thou shouldst make me blessed to consist in that which is Thine own! That Thou shouldst grant me to have not only the sight of Thee, but to share in Thy very own joy! O prepare me for it, teach me to thirst for it.

PLAIN AND PAROCHIAL SERMONS

ON THE ELDER BROTHER

Lo, these many years do I serve thee, neither trans-gressed I at any time thy commandment; and yet thou never gavest me a kid, that I might make merry with my friend. Luke 15:29

The elder brother had always lived at home. He had seen things go on one way, and as natural and right, got attached to them in that one way. But then he could not conceive that they possibly could go on in any other way. He thought he understood his Father's ways and principles far more than he did, and when an occur-rence took place for which he had hitherto met with no precedent, he lost himself, as being suddenly thrust aside out of the small circle in which he had formerly walked. He was disconcerted and angry with his Father.

And so in religion, we have need to watch against that narrowness of mind to which we are tempted by the uniformity and tranquillity of God's providence towards us. We should be on our guard lest we suppose ourselves to have such a clear knowledge of God's ways as to rely implicitly on our own notions and feelings. Men attach an undue importance to this or that point in opinions or practices handed down to them, and cannot understand how God's blessing can be given to modes of acting to which they themselves are unaccustomed. The Jews thought religion would come to an end if the Temple were destroyed, whereas, in fact, it has spread abroad and flourished more marvellously since than ever it did before.

Unwary Christians become not only over-confident of their knowledge of God's ways, but positive in their over-confidence. They do not like to be contradicted in their opinions, and are generally most attached to the very points which are most especially of their own devising. They forget that all of us are at best but learners in the school of Divine Truth, that they themselves ought to be ever learning, and that they may be sure of the truth of their creed without a like assurance in the details of religious opinion. They find it a much more comfortable view to give up seeking, and to believe they have nothing more to find. A right faith is ever eager and on the watch, with quick eyes and ears, for tokens of God's will, whether He should speak through nature or in the way of grace. "I will stand upon my watch, and set me upon the tower, and will watch to see what He will say unto me, and what I shall answer when I am reproved." (Habakkuk 2:1).

But those who have long had God's favor without cloud or storm are apt to presume and to become irreverent. The elder brother was too familiar with his Father. Irreverence is the very opposite temper to faith. "Son, thou art ever with Me, and all I have is thine." This most gracious truth was the very cause of his murmuring. When Christians have but a little, they are thankful; they gladly pick up the crumbs under the table. Give them much, and they soon forget it is much; and when they find it is not all, and that for other men, too, even for penitents, God has some good in store, straightway they are offended. They *act* as if they thought that the Christian privileges belonged to them over others by a sort of fitness. And they like respect to be shown them by the world, and are jealous of anything which is likely to intefere with the continuance of their credit and authority.

Hence such persons are least fitted to deal with difficult times. God works wondrously in the world. Sometimes He brings about good by means of wicked men, or seems to bless the efforts of those who have separated from His holy Church more than those of His true laborers. If the fact is so, we must not resist it, lest we be found fighting against God; nor must we quarrel with it after the manner of the elder brother. We must take everything as God's gift, hold fast our principles, not give them up because appearances are for the moment against them, but believe all things will come round at length. On the other hand, we must not cease to beg of God, and try to gain the spirit of a sound mind, the power to separate truth from falsehood, and to test the spirit, the disposition to submit to God's teaching, and the wisdom to act as the varied course of affairs requires.

Let us then guard against abusing our happy lot
while we have it, or we may lose it for having abused
it. Let us guard against discontent in any shape, and as
we cannot help hearing what goes on in the world, let
us guard, on hearing it, against all intemperate, un-
charitable feelings toward those who differ from us or
oppose us. Let us pray for our enemies; let us try to
make out people to be as good as they can fairly and
safely be considered; let us rejoice at any symptoms of
repentance, or any marks of good principle in those
who are on the side of error. Let us be forgiving. Let us
try to be very humble, to understand our ignorance,
and to rely constantly on the enlightening grace of our
Great Teacher.

(From Plain and Parochial Sermons, Vol. III.)

PROMISING WITHOUT DOING

*A certain man had two sons; and he came to the
first, and said, Son, go work today in my vineyard. He
answered and said, I will not; but afterward he
repented and went. And he came to the second, and
said likewise. And he answered and said, I go, Sir; and
went not."* Matt. 21:28-30.

Our religious professions are at a far greater distance
from our acting upon them than we ourselves are
aware. We know generally that it is our duty to serve
God, and we resolve we will do so faithfully. We are
sincere in this generally desiring and purposing to be
obedient, and we think we are in earnest. Yet we go
away, and presently, without any struggle of mind or

apparent change of purpose, almost without knowing ourselves what we do — we go away and do that which is the very contrary to the resolution we have expressed. This inconsistency is exposed by our blessed Lord in the second part of this parable. You will observe that in the case of the first son, who said he would not go to work, and yet did go, it is said, "afterward he repented." He underwent a positive change of purpose. But in the case of the second, it is merely said, "he answered, I go, Sir; and he went not." Here there was no revolution of sentiment, nothing deliberate; he merely acted according to his habitual frame of mind. He did not go to work because it was contrary to his general character to work; only he did not know this. He said, "I go, Sir," sincerely, from the feeling of the moment; but when the words were out of his mouth, they were forgotten. It was like the wind blowing against a stream, which seems for a moment to change its course in consequence, but in fact flows down as before.

We promise to serve God: we do not perform; and that not from deliberate faithlessness in the particular case, but because it is our nature, our *way* not to obey, and *we* do not know this; we do not know ourselves, or what we are promising.

Take for instance, our mistaking good feelings for real religious principle. Consider how often this takes place. It is often the case with the young who have not been exposed to temptation. They have (we will say) been brought up religiously, they wish to be religious..., but they think themselves far more religious than they really are. They suppose they hate sin and understand the Truth and can resist the world, when they hardly know the meaning of the words they use.

Again, how often is a man incited by circumstances to utter a virtuous wish, or propose a generous or valiant deed, and perhaps applauds himself for his own good feeling, and has no suspicion that he is not able to act upon it. In truth he does not understand where the real difficulty of his duty lies. He takes it for granted he can do what he wishes; but is not conscious of the load of corrupt nature and sinful habits which hang upon his will and clog it in each particular exercise of it. So very difficult is obedience, so hardly won is every step in our Christian course, so sluggish and inert our corrupt nature that I would have a man disbelieve he can do one jot or tittle beyond what he has already done; refrain from borrowing aught on the hope of the future, however good a security for it he seems to be able to show; and never take his good feelings and wishes in pledge for one single untried deed.

We can never answer how we shall act under new circumstances. A very little knowledge of life and our own hearts will teach us this. Men whom we meet in the world turn out, in the course of their trial, so differently from what their former conduct promises; they view things so differently *before* they were tempted and *after*, that we who see and wonder at it, have abundant cause to look to ourselves, not to be high-minded, but to fear. Even the most matured saints, those who imbibed in largest measure the power and fulness of Christ's Spirit, and worked righteousness most diligently in their day, if they could have been thoroughly scanned even by man, would (I am persuaded) have exhibited inconsistencies such as would surprise and shock their most ardent disciples. The best men are uncertain; they are great, and they are little again; they stand firm, and then fall. Such is human virtue.

My object has been to lead you to some true notion of the depths and deceitfulness of the heart which we do not really know. It is easy to speak of human nature as corrupt in the general, to admit it in the general, and then get off the subject; as if the doctrine being once admitted, there was nothing more to be done with it. But in truth we can have no real apprehension of the doctrine of our corruption until we view the structure of our minds, part by part; and dwell upon and draw out the signs of our weakness, inconsistency, and ungodliness, which are such as can arise from nothing else than some strange original defect in our moral nature.

The management of our hearts is quite above us. Under these circumstances, it becomes our comfort to look up to God. He knoweth whereof we are made, and He alone can uphold us. He sees with most appalling distinctness all our sins, all the windings and recesses of evil within us; yet it is our only comfort to know that, and to trust Him for help against ourselves. To those who have a right notion of their weakness, the thought of their Almighty Sanctifier and Guide is continually present. They believe in the necessity of a spiritual influence to change and strengthen them, not as a mere abstract doctrine, but as a practical and most consolatory truth, daily to be fulfilled in their warfare with sin and Satan.

This conviction of our excessive weakness must further lead us to test ourselves continually in little things, ever to be suspicious of ourselves, and not only to refrain from promising much, but actually to put ourselves to the test in order to keep ourselves wakeful.

There is only one place where the Christian allows himself to profess openly, and that is in Church. Here, under the guidance of Apostles and Prophets, he says many things boldly, as speaking after them, and as before Him who searcheth the reins. There can be no harm in professing much directly to God, because *while we speak, we know He sees through our professions, and takes them for what they really are, prayers.* How much, for instance, do we profess when we say the Creed! And in the Collects we put on the full character of a Christian. We desire and seek the best gifts, and declare our strong purpose to serve God with our whole hearts. By doing this, we remind ourselves of our duty, and humble ourselves meanwhile by the taunt (so to call it) of putting upon our dwindled and unhealthy forms those ample and glorious garments which befit the upright and full-grown believer.

(From *Plain and Parochial Sermons,* Vol. 1.)

OBEDIENCE THE REMEDY FOR RELIGIOUS PERPLEXITY

Wait on the Lord, and keep His way, and He shall exalt thee to inherit the land. Psalm 37:34

This Psalm is written with a view of encouraging good men who are in perplexity — and especially perplexity concerning God's designs, providence, and will. "Fret not thyself." This is the lesson it inculcates from first to last. This world is in a state of confusion. Unworthy men prosper, and are looked on as the greatest men of the time. Truth and goodness are thrown into the shade; but wait patiently — "Peace, be still"; in the end, the better side shall triumph — "The meek shall inherit the earth."

The use of difficulties to all of us in our trial in this world is obvious. Our faith is variously assailed by doubts and difficulties in order to prove its sincerity. If we really love God and His Son, we shall go on in spite of opposition, even though He seems to repel us (as with the Canaanite woman). If we are not in earnest, difficulty makes us turn back. This is one of the ways God separates the corn from the chaff, gradually gathering each, as time goes on, into its own heap.

To all those who are perplexed in any way soever, who wish for light but cannot find it, one precept must be given — obey. It is obedience which brings a man into the right path; it is obedience that keeps him there and strengthens him in it. Under all circumstances, whatever be the cause of your distress — obey. In the words of the text, "Wait on the Lord, and keep His way, and He shall exalt thee."

Every science has its difficulties at first; why then should the science of living well be without them? When the subject of religion is new to us, it is strange. We have heard the truths all our lives without feeling them duly; at length, when they affect us, we cannot believe them to be the same we have long known. We are thrown out of our fixed notions of things. An embarrassment ensues. This distrust of ourselves is greater the longer we have been living in inattention to sacred subjects, and the more we are now humbled and ashamed of ourselves. And it leads us to take up with the first religious guide who offers himself to us, whatever his real fitness for the office.

To these agitations of mind about what is truth and what is error, is added an anxiety about ourselves which is apt to lead us wrong. We do not feel, think and act as religiously as we would wish, and while we are sorry for it, we are perhaps also *surprised* at it and impatient at it. Instead of reflecting that we are just beginning our recovery from a most serious disease of long standing, we conceive we ought to be able to trace the course of our recovery by a sensible improvement. We are apt not only to be humbled (which we ought to be) but to be discouraged at the slowness with which we are able to amend, in spite of all the assistance of God's grace. Forgetting that our proper title at very best is that of penitent sinners, we seek to rise all at once into the blessedness of the sons of God.

This impatience leads us to misuse the purpose of self-examination. It is primarily intended to inform us of our sins, whereas we are disappointed if it does not at once tell us of our improvement! Doubtless, in a length of time, we shall be conscious of improvement, too, but the object of ordinary self-examination is to find out whether we are in earnest, and what we have done wrong in order that we may pray for pardon and do better. Further, reading in Scripture how exalted the thoughts and spirit of Christians should be, we are apt to forget that a Christian spirit is the growth of time, and that we cannot force it upon our minds, however desirable and necessary it may be to possess it; that by giving utterance to religious sentiments we do not become religious, rather the reverse. On the other hand, if we strove to obey God's will in all things, we actually should be gradually training our hearts into the fullness of the Christian spirit. But not understanding this, men are led to speak much and expressly upon sacred subjects, as if it were a duty to do so, and in hope of its making them better. When they cannot sustain these to that height which they consider almost the characteristic of a true Christian, they are discouraged and tempted to despair. Added to this, sometimes their old sins, reviving from the slumber into which they have been cast for a time, rush over their minds and seem to take them captive.

Now such persons must be reminded first of all, of the greatness of the work which they have undertaken, namely, the sanctification of their souls. Those indeed who think this is an easy task, or think it will be easy for them because God's grace will take all the toil of it from them, must be disappointed on finding by experience the force of their original evil nature, and the extreme slowness with which a Christian is able to improve it. And it is to be feared that this disappointment in some cases results in a belief that it is *impossible* to overcome our evil selves; that bad as we are, bad we must be; that our innate corruption lies like a load on our hearts and no more admits of improvement than a stone does of light and thought, and that, in consequence, all we have to do is to believe in Christ who is to save us, and to dwell on the thoughts of His perfect work for us — that this is all we can do — and that it is presumption as well as folly to attempt more.

But what says the text? "Wait on the Lord and keep His way." St. Paul says, "I can do all things through Christ which strengtheneth me." The very fruit of Christ's passion was the gift of the Holy Spirit, which was to enable us to do what otherwise we could not do — "to work out our own salvation." Yet while we must aim at this, and feel convinced of our ability to do it at length through the gifts bestowed on us, we cannot do it rightly without a deep settled conviction of the exceeding difficulty of the work. That is, not only shall we be tempted to negligence, but to impatience, and thence into all kinds of unlawful treatments of the soul, if we are possessed by a notion that religious discipline soon becomes easy to the believer and the heart is speedily changed.

Let every beginner, then, make up his mind to suffer disquiet and perplexity. He cannot complain that it should be thus; and though he be deeply ashamed of himself that it is so, still he has no cause to be surprised or discouraged. The more he makes up his mind manfully to bear doubt, struggle against it, and meekly to do God's will all through it, the sooner this unsettled state of mind will cease, and order will rise out of confusion. "Wait on the Lord," this is the rule; "keep His way," this is the manner of the waiting. Go about your duty; mind little things as well as great. Do not pause and say, "I am as I was; day after day passes, and still no light." Go on. It is very painful to be haunted by wandering doubts, to have thoughts shoot across the mind about the reality of religion altogether, or of this or that particular doctrine of it or about the correctness of one's own faith. But it must be right to serve God; we have a voice within us answering to the injunction of the text, of waiting on Him and keeping His way. And surely such obedient waiting upon Him will obtain His blessing. "Blessed are they that keep His commandments."

It is from God's great goodness that our daily, constant study is in the performance of small and comparatively easy services. To be dutiful and obedient in ordinary matters, to speak the truth, to be honest, to be sober, to keep from sinful words and thoughts, to be kind and forgiving — and all this for our Savior's sake — let us attempt *these* duties first. *They* even will be difficult — the least of them; still they are much easier than the solution of the doubts which harass us, and they will by degrees give us a practical knowledge of the Truth.

When we set about to obey God in the ordinary businesses of daily life, we are at once interested by realities which withdraw our minds from vague fears and uncertain guesses about the future. Without laying aside the thoughts of Christ, still we learn to view Him in His tranquil providence before we set about contemplating His greater works, and we are saved from taking an unchristian thought for the morrow while we are busied in present services. Thus our Savior gradually discloses Himself to the troubled mind.

Whatever our difficulty be, this is plain. "Wait on the Lord, and keep His way, and He shall exalt thee." Or in our Savior's words: "He that hath My commandments and keepeth them, he it is that loveth Me; and he that loveth Me shall be loved of My Father, and I will love Him and will manifest Myself to him." (John 14:21).

(From *Plain and Parochial Sermons*, Vol. I.)

REMEMBRANCE OF PAST MERCIES

I am not worthy of the least of all the mercies, and of all the truth which Thou hast shown unto Thy servant. Genesis 32:10

The spirit of humble thankfulness for past mercies which these words imply is a grace to which we are especially called in the Gospel. Jacob, who spoke them, knew not of those great and wonderful acts of love with which God has since visited the race of man. But though he might not know the depths of God's counsels, he knew himself well enough to know that he was worthy of no good things, whereas he had deserved evil; and truth, in that He had made him promises, and had been faithful to them. In consequence, he overflowed with gratitude when he looked back upon the past; marvelling at the contrast between what he was in himself and what God had been to him.

Such thankfulness, I say, is eminently a Christian grace and is enjoined on us in the New Testament. We are exhorted to be thankful and to let "the word of Christ dwell in us richly in all wisdom, teahcing and admonishing one another in psalms and hymns and spiritual songs, singing with grace in our hearts to the Lord." (Col. 3:15, 16).

Jacob's distinguishing grace then, as I think it may be called, was a habit of affectionate musing upon God's providences towards him in times past, and of overflowing thankfulness for them. This seems to have been his distinguishing grace. All good men have in their measure all graces; for He, by whom they have any, does not give one apart from the whole: He gives the root, and the root puts forth branches. But since time and circumstances, and their own use of the gift, and their own disposition and character have much influence on the mode of its manifestation, so it happens that each good man has his own distinguishing grace, apart from the rest, his own particular hue and fragrance and fashion, as a flower may have.

Abraham, for instance, was the pattern of faith. He left his country at God's word; and, at the same word, took up the knife to slay his own son. Abraham seems to have had something very noble and magnanimous about him. He could realize and make present to him things unseen. He followed God in the dark as promptly and as firmly, with as cheerful a heart and bold a steeping, as if he were in broad daylight. There is something very great in this. St. Paul calls Abraham *our* father, for we are bound to walk by faith, not by sight; and are blessed in faith, and justified in faith, as was faithful Abraham.

Now that faith in which Abraham excelled was not Jacob's characteristic excellence. Not that he had not faith, and great faith, else he would not have been so dear to God. However, Jacob's faith, earnest and vigorous as it was, was not like Abraham's. Abraham kept his affections loose from everything earthly, and was ready, at God's word, to slay his only son. Jacob had many sons, and may we not even say that he indulged them overmuch? Even as regards Joseph, whom he so deservedly loved, beautiful and touching as his love of him is, yet there is a great contrast between his feelings towards the "sons of his old age" and those of Abraham towards Isaac, the unexpected offspring of his hundredth year — and not only such, but his long-promised only son, with whom were the promises. Again, Abraham left his country — so did Jacob; but Abraham, at God's word — Jacob from necessity on the threat of Esau. Abraham, from the first, felt that God was his portion and his inheritance, and in a great and generous spirit, he freely gave up all he had, being sure that he should find what was more excellent in doing so. But Jacob, in spite of his really living by faith, wished, as one passage of his history shows, to see before he fully believed. When he was escaping from Esau and came to Bethel, and God appeared to him in a dream and gave him promises, but not yet the performance of them — what did he do? Did he simply accept them? He says, "*If* God will be with me, and will keep me in this way that I go, and will give me bread to eat, and raiment to put on, so that I come again to my father's house in peace, *then* shall the Lord be my God." (Gene. 28:20,21) He makes his obedience, in some sense, depend on a condition; and although we must not, and need not, take the words as if he meant that he would not serve God *till* and *unless* He did for him what He had promised, yet they seem to show fear and anxiety, gentle indeed, and subdued, and very human, yet an anxiety which Abraham had not. We feel Jacob to be more like ourselves than Abraham was.

What, then, was Jacob's distinguishing grace, as faith was Abraham's? I have already said it: I suppose, thankfulness. Abraham appears ever to have been looking forward in *hope* — Jacob looking back in *memory:* the one setting his affections on the future, the other on the past; the one making his way towards the promises, the other musing over their fulfillment. Of course Abraham did look back also, and Jacob, as he says on his death bed, waited "on the salvation of God." But this was the difference between them: Abraham was a hero, Jacob "a plain man, dwelling in tents."

Jacob seems to have had a gentle, tender, affectionate, timid mind — easily frightened, easily agitated, loving God so much that he feared to lose Him. Were it not for faith, love would become impatient, and thus Jacob desired to possess, not from cold incredulity or hardness of heart, but from such a loving impatience. Such men are easily downcast, and must be treated kindly; they soon despond, they shrink from the world, for they feel its rudeness, which bolder natures do not. Neither Abraham nor Jacob loved the world. But Abraham did not fear, did not feel it. Jacob felt and winced, as being wounded by it. You recollect his touching complaints, "All these things are against me!" — "Then you shall bring down my grey hairs with sorrow to the grave." Elsewhere we are told, "All his sons and all his daughters rose up to comfort him, but he refused to be comforted." You see what a child-like, sensitive, sweet mind he had. Accordingly, his happiness lay, not in looking forward to the hope, but backwards upon the experience of God's mercies towards him. He delighted to trace and gratefully to acknowledge what he had been given, leaving the future to itself.

After he had returned to his own land, he proceeded to fulfill the promise he had made to consecrate Bethel as a house of God, "Let us arise and go up to Bethel; and I will make there an altar unto God, *who answered me in the day of my distress, and was with me in the way which I went.*" And further on, when he speaks of waiting for God's salvation, which is an act of hope, he so words it as at the same time to dwell upon the past: "I *have* waited," he says, that is, all my life long, "I have waited for Thy salvation, O Lord." (Gen. 49:18) Such was Jacob, living in memory rather than in hope, counting times, recording seasons, keeping days; having his history by heart, and his past life in his hand.

Well were it for us if we had the character of mind shown in Jacob, the temper of dependence upon God's providence and thankfulness under it, and careful memory of all He has done for us. It would be well if we were in the habit of looking at all we have as God's gift, undeservedly given, and day by day continued to us solely by His mercy. He gave; He may take away. He gave us all we have, life, health, strength, reason, enjoyment, the light of conscience; whatever we have good and holy within us; whatever faith we have; whatever of a renewed will; whatever love towards Him; whatever power over ourselves; whatever prospect of heaven. He gave us relatives, friends, education, training, knowledge, the Bible, the Church. All comes from Him. He gave, He may take away. If He should take away, we should be called on to follow Job's pattern, and be resigned: "The Lord gave, the Lord hath taken away. Blessed be the Name of the Lord." While He continues His blessings, we should follow David and Jacob, by living in constant praise and thanksgiving, and in offering up to Him of His own.

We are not our own, any more than what we possess is our own. We did not make ourselves; we cannot be supreme over ourselves. We cannot be our own masters. We are God's property by creation, by redemption, by regeneration. He has a triple claim upon us.

Let us then view God's providences towards us more religiously than we have hitherto done. Let us try to gain a truer view of what we are, and where we are in His kingdom. Let us humbly and reverently attempt to trace His guiding hand in the years which we have hitherto lived. Let us thankfully commemorate the many mercies He has vouchsafed to us in time past, the many sins He has not remembered, the many dangers He has averted, the many prayers He has answered, the many mistakes He has corrected, the many warnings, the many lessons, the much light, the abounding comfort which He has from time to time given. Let us dwell upon times and seasons, times of trouble, times of joy, times of trial, times of refreshment. How did He cherish us as children! How did He guide us in that dangerous time when the mind began to think for itself, and the heart to open to the world! How did He with His sweet discipline restrain our passions, mortify our hopes, calm our fears, enliven our heaviness, sweeten our desolateness, and strengthen our infirmities! How did He gently guide us towards the straight gate! How did He allure us along His everlasting way, in spite of His strictness, in spite of its loneliness, in spite of the dim twilight in which it lay! He has been all things to us. He has been, as He was to Abraham, Isaac, and Jacob, our God, our Shield, our great reward, promising and per-

forming, day by day. "Hitherto hath He helped us."
"He hath been mindful of us and He will bless us." He
has not made us for nought; He has brought us thus far,
in order to bring us further, in order to bring us to the
end. He will never leave us nor forsake us; so that we
may boldly say, "The Lord is my Helper; I will not fear
what flesh can do unto me." We may "cast all our care
upon Him who careth for us." What is it to us how our
future path lies, if it be but His path? What is it to us
whither it leads us, as long as in the end it leads to
Him? What does it matter to us what He puts on us, as
long as He enables us to undergo it with a pure conscience, a true heart, not desiring anything of this world
in comparison of Him? What is it to us what terror
befalls us, if He be but at hand to protect and
strengthen us? "Thou, Israel," He says, "art My servant
Jacob, whom I have chosen, the seed of Abraham My
friend." "Fear not, thou worm Jacob, and ye men of
Israel; I will help thee, saith the Lord and thy
Redeemer, the Holy one of Israel." (Isaiah 41:8, 14).

From *Plain and Parochial Sermons*, Vol. V.

LOVE, THE ONE THING NEEDFUL

*Though I speak with the tongues of men and of
angels, and have not charity, I am become as sounding
brass, or a tinkling cymbal.* I Corinthians 13:1

I suppose the greater number of persons who try to
live Christian lives, and who observe themselves with
any care, are dissatisfied with their own state at this
point, viz. that, whatever their religious attainments

may be, yet they feel that their motive is not the highest — that the love of God, and of man for His sake, is not their ruling principle. They may do much, nay, if it so happens, they may suffer much; but they have little reason to think that they love much; that they do and suffer for love's sake. I do not mean that they thus express themselves exactly, but that they are dissatisfied with themselves. They may call themselves cold, or hard-hearted, or fickle, or double-minded, or doubting, or dim-sighted, or weak in resolve, but they mean pretty much the same things, that their affections do not rest on Almighty God as their great Object. Their reason and their heart do not go together; their reason tending heavenwards, and their heart earthwards. A careful consideration of this defect may serve as one step towards its removal.

Love, and love only, is the fulfilling of the Law, and they only are in God's favor in whom the righteousness of the Law is fulfilled. This we know full well; yet, alas! at the same time, we cannot deny that whatever good thing we have to show, whether activity, or patience, or faith, or fruitfulness in good works, love to God and man is not ours, or, at least, in very scanty measure; not at all proportionately to our apparent attainments. In the first place, love clearly does not consist merely in great sacrifices. We can take no comfort to ourselves that we are God's own merely on the ground of great deeds of great sufferings. The greatest sacrifices without love would be nothing worth, and that they are great does not necessarily prove they are done with love. St. Paul emphatically assures us that his acceptance with God did not stand in any of those high endowments which strike us in him at first sight. One of his highest gifts, for instance, was his spiritual knowledge. He shared and felt the sinfulness and infirmities of human nature; he had a deep insight into the glories of God's grace, such as no natural man can have. He had an awful sense of the realities of heaven, and of the mysteries revealed. He could have answered ten thousand questions on theological subjects, which we now long to ask him. He was a man whom one could not come near without going away wiser than one came: a fountain of knowledge and wisdom ever full, ever approachable, ever flowing, from which all who come in faith gained a measure of the gifts which God had lodged in him. His presence inspired resolution, confidence, and zeal. Such was the great servant of Christ and teacher of the Gentiles; yet he says, "Though I speak with the tongues of men and of angels, though I have the gift of prophecy, and understand all mysteries, and all knowledge, and have not charity, I am become a sounding brass or a tinkling cymbal . . . I am nothing." Spiritual discernment, an insight into the Gospel covenant, is no evidence of love.

Another distinguishing mark of his character, as viewed in Scripture, is his faith, a prompt, decisive, simple assent to God's word, a deadness to motives of earth, a firm hold of the truths of the unseen world, and keenness in following them out; yet he says of his faith also, "Though I have all faith, so that I could remove mountains, and have not charity, I am nothing." Faith is no necessary evidence of love.

A tender consideration of the temporal wants of his brethren is another striking feature of his character, as it is a special characteristic of every true Christian; yet he says, "Though I bestow all my goods to feed the poor, and have not charity, it profiteth me nothing." Self-denying almsgiving is no necessary evidence of love.

Once more. He, if any man, had the spirit of a martyr; yet he implies that even martyrdom, viewed in itself, is no passport into the heavenly kingdom. "Though I give my body to be burned, and have not charity, it profiteth me nothing." Martyrdom is no necessary evidence of love.

I do not say that at this day we have many specimens or much opportunity of such high deeds and attainments; but in our degree we certainly may follow St. Paul in them — in spiritual discernment, in faith, in works of mercy, and in confession. We may, we ought to follow him. Yet though we do, still it may be that we do not possess the one thing needful, the spirit of love, or in a very poor measure, and this is what serious men feel in their own case.

Let us consider the humbler and continual duties of daily life; and see whether they too may not be performed with considerable exactness, yet with deficient love. Surely they may; and serious men complain of themselves here, even more than when they are exercised on greater subjects. Our Lord says, "If you love Me, keep My commandment." But they feel that though they are, to a certain point, keeping God's commandments, yet love is not proportionate, doe not keep pace with their obedience; that obedience springs from some source short of love. This they perceive; they feel themselves to be hollow; a fair outside without a spirit within.

It is possible to obey, not from love towards God and man, but from a sort of conscientiousness short of love; from some notion of acting up to a *law;* that is, more from the fear of God than from love of Him. Surely this is what, in one shape or another, we see daily on all sides of us: the case of men living to the world, yet not without a certain sense of religion, which acts as a restraint on them. They pursue ends of this world, but not to the full; they are checked, and go a certain way only, because they dare not go further. This external restraint acts with various degrees of strength on various persons. They all live to this world, and act from the love of it; they allow their love of the world a certain range; but, at some particular point, which is often quite arbitrary, this man stops, and that man stops. Each stops at a different point in the course of the world, and thinks everyone else profane who goes further, and superstitious who does not go so far — laughs at the latter, is shocked at the former. And hence those few who are miserable enough to have rid themselves of all scruples, look with great contempt on such of their companions as have any, whether those scruples more or less, as being inconsistent and absurd. Scruples at all (be they many or few), proceeding on no rule, and having no evidence of its authority, to claim our respect, they regard scruples as a weakness in our nature, rather than an essential portion of that nature viewed in its perfection and entireness. And since this is all the notion their experience gives them of religion, (not knowing really religious men) they think of religion only as a principle which interferes with our enjoyments unintelligibly and irrationally.

Man is made to love. They see that clearly and truly; but religion, as far as they conceive of it, is a system without objects of love; a system of fear. It repels and forbids, and thus seems to destroy the proper function of man, to be unnatural. And it is true that this sort of fear of God, or rather slavish dread, as it may more truly be called, *is* unnatural; but then it is not religion. Religion consists, not in the mere fear of God, but in His love; or if it be religion, it is but the religion of devils, who believe and tremble; or of idolators, whom devils have seduced, and whose worship is superstition — the attempt to appease beings whom they love not; and, in a word, the religion of the children of this world, who would, if possible serve God *and* Mammon, and, since religion consists of love *and* fear, they give to God their fear, and to Mammon their love.

And what takes place so generally in the world at large, serious men will feel as happening, in its degree, in their own case. They will understand that even strict obedience is no evidence of fervent love, and they will lament to perceive that they obey God far more than they love Him. The thought will come over them as a perplexity, What proof they have that they are not, after all, deceiving themselves and thinking themselves religious when they are not? They will indeed be aware of the sacrifice of their own wishes and pursuits they make to the will of God; but they are conscious also that they sacrifice them because they know they *ought* to do so, not simply from love of God. And they ask, almost in a kind of despair, "How are we to learn, not merely to obey, but to love?"

They say, "How are we to fulfill St. Paul's words, 'The life which I now live in the flesh I live by the faith of the Son of God, who loved me and gave Himself for me'?" And this would seem an especial difficulty in the case of those whose duties lie amid the engagements of this world's business, whose thoughts, affections, exertions, are directed towards things present and temporal. In their case it seems to be a great thing, even if their *rule* of life is a heavenly one, if they *act* according to God's will; but how can they hope that heavenly Objects should fill their heart, when there is no room left for them? How shall things absent displace things present, things unseen the things that are visible? Thus they seem to be reduced, as if by a sort of necessity, to that state of having their hearts set on the world, and being only restrained outwardly by religious rules.

Generally speaking, men will be able to bring against themselves positive charges of lack of love, more unsatisfactory still. I suppose most men, or at least a great number of them, have to lament over their hardness of heart, which is nothing else but the absence of love. I mean that hardness which, for instance, makes us unable to repent as we wish. No repentance is truly such without love; it is love which gives it its efficacy in God's sight. Without love there may be remorse, regret, self-reproach, self-condemnation, but there is no saving penitence. There may be conviction of the reason, but not conversion of the heart. A great many men lament in themselves this lack of love in repenting; they are hard-hearted; they are deeply conscious of their sins; they abhor them; and yet they can take as lively interest in what goes on around them as if they had no such consciousness; or they mourn this minute, and the next are quite impenetrable. Or, though, as they think and believe, they fear God's anger, and are full of confusion at themselves, yet they find (to their surprise, I may say), that they cannot abstain from any indulgence ever so trivial, which would be (as their reason tells them) a natural way of showing sorrow. They eat and drink with as good a heart as if they had no distress upon their minds; they find no difficulty in entering into any of the recreations or secular enjoyments which come in their way. They sleep as soundly; and, in spite of their grief, perhaps find it most difficult to persuade themselves to rise early to pray for pardon. These are signs of lack of love.

Or, again, they have a general indisposition towards prayer and other exercises of devotion. They find it most difficult to get themselves to pray; most difficult, too, to rouse their minds to attend to their prayers. At very best they do but feel satisfaction in devotion *while* they are engaged in it. Then perhaps they find a real pleasure in it, but if any chance throws them out of their habitual exercises, they find it most difficult to return to them. They do not like them well enough to seek them *from* liking them. They are kept in them by habit, by regularity in observing them; not by love. Here, again, is obedience, more or less mechanical, or without love.

Again — a like absence of love is shown in our proneness to be taken up and engrossed with trifles. Why is it that we are so open to the power of excitement? What is it that we are looking out for novelties? Why is it that we complain of lack of variety in a religious life? Why that we cannot bear to go on in an ordinary round of duties year after year? Why do we need powerful preaching, or interesting and touching books in order to keep our thoughts and feelings on God? Why are we so afraid of worldly events or the opinions of men? Why do we so dread their censure or ridicule? — Clearly because we are deficient in love. He who loves cares little for anything else. The world may go as it will. His thoughts are drawn another way; he is solicitous mainly to walk with God and to be found with God, and is in perfect peace because he is stayed on Him.

And here is another proof of how weak our love is: how inadequate our professed principles are found to be to support us in affliction. I suppose it often happens to men to feel this when some reverse or unexpected distress comes upon them. Indeed they will feel it most who have let their words, nay their thoughts, much outrun their hearts. But many feel it too, who have tried to make their reason and affections keep pace with each other. We are told of the righteous man, that "he will not be afraid of any evil tidings, for his heart standeth fast, and believeth in the Lord. His heart is established, and will not shrink." (Psalm 112:7,8). Such must be the case of everyone who realizes his own words, when he talks of the shortness of life, the wearisomeness of the world, and the security of heaven. Yet how cold and dreary do all such topics prove to be when one comes into trouble! And why, except that he has been after all set upon things visible, not on God, while he has been speaking of things invisible? There has been much profession and little love.

These are some of the proofs which are continually brought home to us of our lack of love to God. They will readily suggest others to us.

What causes this evil? I must say plainly, strange as it may appear at first sight, that the comforts of life are the main cause of it; and, much as we may lament and struggle against it, till we learn to dispense with them in good measure, we shall not overcome it. Till we, in a certain sense, detach ourselves from our bodies, our minds will not be in a state to receive divine impressions, and to exert heavenly aspirations. A smooth and easy life, an uninterrupted enjoyment of the goods of Providence, full meals, soft raiment, well-furnished homes, the pleasures of sense, the feeling of security, the consciousness of wealth — these, and the like, if we are not careful, choke up all the avenues of the soul through which the the light and breath of heaven might come to us. A hard life is, alas! no certain method of becoming spiritually minded, but it is one out of the means by which Almighty God makes us so. We must, at least at seasons, defraud ourselves of nature, if we would not be defrauded of grace. If we attempt to force our minds into a loving and devotional temper without this preparation, it is too plain what will follow — the grossness and coarseness, the affectation, the effeminacy, the unreality, the presumption, the hollowness (suffer me to say plainly but seriously what I mean), in a word, what Scripture calls Hypocrisy, which we see around us; that state of mind in which the reason, seeing what we should be, and the conscience enjoining it, and the heart being unequal to it, some or other pretense is set up by way of compromise, so that men may say, "Peace, peace, when there is no peace."

Next, after urging this habitual preparation of heart, let me bid you cherish what otherwise it would be shocking to attempt, a constant sense of the love of your Lord and Savior in dying on the Cross for you. "The love of Christ," says the Apostle, "constraineth us." Gratitude does not always lead to love, for we often reproach ourselves for not loving loving persons who have loved us, but where hearts are in some measure renewed after Christ's image, there, under His grace, gratitude to Him will increase our love of Him. Here, again, self-discipline will be necessary. It makes the heart tender as well as reverent. Christ showed His love in deed, not in word, and you will be touched by the thought of His Cross far more by bearing it after Him than by glowing accounts of it. All the ways in which you bring it before you must be simple and severe. "Excellency of speech" or "enticing words," to use St. Paul's language, is the worst way of any. Think of the Cross when you rise and when you lie down, when you go out and when you come in, when you eat and when you walk and when you talk, when you buy and when you sell, when you labor and when you rest, consecrating and sealing all your doings with this one mental action, the thought of the Crucified. Do not talk of it to others; be silent, like the penitent woman who "stood at His feet behind Him weeping, and began to wash His feet with tears, and did wipe them with the hairs of her head, and kissed His feet and anointed them with ointment." Christ said of her, "Her sins, which are many, are forgiven her, for she loved much. . . ." (Luke 7:38, 47).

Let us dwell often upon His manifold mercies to us and to our brethren: His adorable counsels, as manifested in our personal election — how it is that we are called and others are not; the wonders of His grace towards us, from our infancy until now; the gifts He has given us; the aid He has vouchsafed; the answers He has accorded to our prayers; what unexpected events have worked His purposes; how evil has been changed into good; how His sacred truth has ever been preserved unimpaired; how Saints have been brought on to their perfection in the darkest times.

It is by such deeds and such thoughts that our services, our repentings, our prayers, our intercourse with men will become permeated with the spirit of love. We will do everything thankfully and joyfully when we are temples of Christ, with His Image set up in us. Then we can mix with the world without loving it, for our affections are given to another. We can bear to look on the world's beauty, for we have no heart for it. We are not disturbed by its frowns, for we do not live in its smiles. We rejoice in the House of Prayer because He is there "whom our soul loveth." We can condescend to the poor and lowly, for they are the presence of Him who is Invisible. We are patient in bereavement, adversity, or pain, for they are tokens of Christ's presence. May we seek and find love more and more, the older we grow, till death comes and gives us the sight of Him who is at once its Object and its Author.

(Sermon #3, Book 5, *Plain and Parochial Sermons*, abridged.)

MORNING AND EVENING
From St. Gregory Nazianzen

Morning

I rise and raise my clasped hands to Thee!
Henceforth, the darkness hath no part in me,
Thy sacrifice this day;
Abiding firm, and with a freeman's might
Stemming the waves of passion in the fight;
Ah, should I from Thee stray,
My hoary head, Thy table where I bow,
Will be my shame, which are mine honor now.
Thus I set out; — Lord, lead me on my way!

Evening

O holiest Truth! How have I lied to Thee!
I vowed this day Thy festival should be:
But I am dim ere night.
Surely I made my prayer, and I did deem
That I could keep me in Thy morning beam,
Immaculate and bright.
But my foot slipped, and as I lay, he came,
My gloomy foe, and robbed me of heaven's flame.
Help Thou my darkness, Lord, till I am light.

(1834. Oxford.)

ABRAHAM

But Abram said to the king of Sodom, "I have sworn to the Lord God Most High, Maker of heaven and earth, that I would not take a thread or a sandal-thong or anything that is yours, lest you should say, 'I have made Abram rich.'" Genesis 14:22, 23.

The better portion didst thou choose, Great Heart,
Thy God's first choice, and pledge of Gentile grace!
Faith's truest type, he with unruffled face
Bore the world's smile and bade her slaves depart;
Whether, a trader with no trader's art,
He buys in Canaan his last resting-place —
Or freely yields rich Siddim's[1] ample space, —
Or braves the rescue and the battle's smart,
Yet scorns the heathen gifts of those he saved.

O happy is their souls' high solitude
Who thus commune with God and not with earth!
Amid the scoffings of the wealth-enslaved,
A ready prey, as though in absent mood
They calmly disregard th'unmannered mirth.
                              (At Sea. 1832.)

---

[1] An alternate form of *Sodom*.

PRAISE TO THE HOLIEST

Praise to the Holiest in the height,
And in the depth be praise;
In all His words most wonderful,
Most sure in all His ways.

O loving wisdom of our God!
When all was sin and shame,
A second Adam to the fight
And to the rescue came.

O wisest love! that flesh and blood,
Which did in Adam fail,
Should strive afresh against the foe,
Should strive, and should prevail;

And that a higher gift than grace
Should flesh and blood refine:
God's presence and His very Self
And Essence all divine.

O generous love! that He who smote
In Man for man the foe,
The double agony in Man
For man should undergo;

And in the garden secretly,
And on the Cross on high,
Should teach His brethren and inspire
To suffer and to die.

Praise to the Holiest in the height,
And in the depth be praise;
In all His words most wonderful,
Most sure in all His ways!

(From The Dream of Gerontius.)

SEMITA JUSTORUM

When I look back upon my former race,
Season I see at which the inward Ray
More brightly burned, or guided some new way:
Truth, in its wealthier scene and nobler space
Given for my eye to range and feet to trace.

And next I mark, 'twas trial did convey,
Or grief, or pain, or strange eventful day,
To my tormented soul such larger grace.

So now, whene'er in journeying on I feel
The shadow of the Providential Hand,
Deep breathless stirrings shoot across my breast,
Searching to know what He will now reveal,
What sin uncloak, what stricter rule command,
And girding me to work His full behest.

(At Sea, June 25, 1833)

SENSITIVENESS

Time was, I shrank from what was right
For fear of what was wrong;
I would not brave the sacred fight,
Because the foe was strong.

But now I cast that finer sense
And sorer shame aside;
Such dread of sin was indolence,
Such aim at Heaven was pride.

So, when my Savior calls, I rise,
And calmly do my best;
Leaving to Him, with silent eyes
Of hope and fear, the rest.

I step, I mount where He has led;
Men count my haltings o'er;—
I know them; yet, though self I dread,
I love His precept more.

DESOLATION

Oh, say not thou art left of God
Because His tokens[1] in the sky
Thou canst not read: this earth He trod
To teach thee He was ever nigh.

He sees, beneath the fig-tree green,
Nathanael read His sacred lore;
Shouldst thou thy chamber seek, unseen,
He enters through the unopen'd door.

And when thou liest, by slumber bound,
Outwearied in the Christian fight,
In glory, girt with saints around,
He stands above thee through the night.

When friends to Emmaus bend their course,
He joins, although He holds their eyes:
Or, shouldst thou feel some fever's force,
He takes thy hand, He bids thee rise.

Or on a voyage, when calms prevail,
And prison thee upon the sea,
He walks the wave, He wings the sail,
The shore is gained, and thou art free.

(1833. Off Sardinia)

---

[1]The word *token* is often used in reference to human difficulties and trials,
meaning a distinguishing sign of God's authority and presence in our lives.

VEXATIONS

Each trial has its weight; which, whoso bears
Knows his own woe, and need of succoring grace;
The martyr's hope half wipes away the trace
Of flowing blood; the while life's humblest cares
Smart more, because they hold in Holy Writ no place.

This be my comfort in these days of grief,
Which is not Christ's, nor forms heroic tale.
Apart from Him, if not a sparrow fail,
May not He pitying view, and send relief
When foes or friends perplex, and peevish thoughts
    prevail?

Then keep good heart, nor take the faithless course
Of Thomas, who must see ere he would trust.
Faith will fill up God's Word — not poorly, just
To the bare letter, heedless of its force,
But walking by its light amid earth's sun and dust.
              (June 21, 1833. Off Sardinia)

HUMILIATION

I have been honor'd and obey'd,
I have met scorn and slight;
And my heart loves earth's sober shade
More than her laughing light.

For what is rule but a sad weight
Of duty and a snare?
What meanness[1], but a happier fate
The Savior's cross to share?

This my hid choice, if not from heaven,
Moves on the heavenward line;
Cleanse it, good Lord, from earthly leaven,
And make it simply Thine.

[1] Meanness = destitute of distinction; common; humble.

LEAD, KINDLY LIGHT

John Henry Cardinal Newman: 1801-1890

A Personal Word

So much has been written in recent years about the life, work and thought of Cardinal Newman that a neophyte hesitates to add anything of one's own. In order to acquaint those who know little or nothing about him, however, it seems appropriate to give a sketch of some of the more outstanding features of his life. Those who wish to delve further into it are referred to the books listed in the bibliography.

In this present essay, in addition to giving some of the facts, I am offering a personal interpretation of a spiritual dimension which I have not seen in other works. Viewed from the standpoint of the way God deals with His children, one can see something other than mere human agencies or accidents of history in the life of John Henry Newman. Because he, too, viewed his life as coming from God and under God's hand, it seems helpful to look and see the circumstances of his life as ways in which God was dealing with him. Seeing that can help us better understand some of the things in our own lives that may otherwise remain unsolved mysteries and unwelcome stumbling blocks.

It is not surprising that the life of a man that covered almost the entire 19th century should be marked by some paradoxes. For the century itself — certainly one of the most remarkable in human history — was a century of rapid and radical change.

The England into which John Henry Newman was born on February 21, 1801, was struggling with its recent colonial losses in North America and with its recurrent wars with France — first under the Revolutionary radicals, and later under Napoleon. George III still reigned between successive bouts of madness. In that same year, 1801, the United Kingdom of Great Britain and Ireland was formed. The Church of England and the Church of Ireland were united as one Church (Protestant), and no concession was made to the Roman Catholic population of Ireland.

John was the oldest of six children, the son of a London banker, John Newman. His mother, Jemima Fourdrinier, was a descendant of French Huegenots from the 18th century. The Newman family suffered financial reverses in the depression that followed the Napoleonic wars, but in spite of this, John was sent to school to prepare for the University.

Although the Newmans were "moderate Church of England" in their religious views, the school to which John was sent was conducted by a clergyman with definite Evangelical and Calvinist leanings. As a child, John had shown a keen interest in books, music, theatrics, boating, walking and riding. His love of the violin would be renewed in later life to his great comfort and enjoyment. It also happened that in his reading John had run across books and tracts which questioned the existence of God, the immortality of the soul and the veracity of the Bible. Swayed by these opinions, he had early on determined to be "virtuous but not religious."

In 1816, however, two significant events took place. His father's bank failed and closed its doors on March 16th. While the London home was being vacated and the rest of the family was getting settled in new quarters at Alton, John was sent back to Ealing for the summer. There he became ill, the first of three significant illnesses in his life. At Ealing, one of the newer teachers, a young, serious-minded clergyman, Rev. Walter Mayers, often talked with him about spiritual things. In his *Apologia*, Newman writes appreciatively, that Mr. Mayers "was the human means of [the] beginning of divine faith in me." It was in that setting at the age of fifteen that John experienced a profound conversion to God. Writing about it forty-three years later, he called it that "inward conversion of which I was conscious (and of which I am still more certain than that I have hands and feet)...." Somewhat to his parents' discomfort (especially his father's), Newman had become a conscious and ardent Evangelical. Writing in his private journal that year, he said, "Thy wonderful grace turned me right round when I was more like a devil than a wicked boy." God had mercifully touched his heart and drawn him from agnosticism and impiety.

In December, 1816, he entered Trinity College, Oxford, planning to train for the law. A close friendship developed between him and John William Bowden which lightened the three years of study there. Again, in his journal, Newman wrote "Whereas I was proud, self-righteous, impure, abominable and altogether corrupt in my sinful imagination, Thou wast pleased to turn me from such a state of darkness and irreligion by a mercy which is too wonderful for me, and to make me fall down humbled and abased before Thy footstool. O merciful Savior, continue Thy grace and let me so run the race that is set before me that I may lay hold on everlasting life; let me be a faithful soldier."[1]

Recalling this period long after he had left behind many of his distinctly Evangelical and Calvinistic beliefs, he could not recall that those beliefs (or opinions, as he called them) led him to be careless about pleasing God. He had held firmly, he says, to the belief in heaven and hell, divine favor and divine wrath, of the justified and the unjustified.[2]

At the end of his three years at Trinity, he failed his first attempt at the scholarship examination for a fellowship. Humiliated and overwhelmed, he allowed the failure to further crucify his ambition and latent vanity. Chastened and sobered, he began to think of taking Holy Orders and made plans to remain at Oxford as a student and tutor until he was old enough to be ordained.

Because he later tore out and threw away most of the early entries in his journal, it is impossible to reconstruct the details of this Evangelical period of Newman's spiritual odyssey much beyond the scant treatment he gives it in his *Apologia*. It is of interest to many, because even through his subsequent pilgrimage through the edges of Anglican liberalism, Anglo-Catholicism to Roman Catholicism, he never lost the warmth and personal commitment he experienced in his original conversion. Remarkable, too, is that in his earliest period as a conscious Christian, he felt a call to live a single, celibate life — a fact that is even more remarkable in that such a state was generally considered odd or unhealthy by the Evangelicals of the time. He aspired to mission work and continued to read Evangelical theology seriously. At home, both of his parents were concerned about his over-zealous religious activity. His younger brother, Francis, too, had come under Mr. Mayer's influence at Ealing, and experienced a conversion. Concerning his mother, John wrote, "She seemed to think I was righteous overmuch, and was verging on enthusiasm. I was also leading Francis with me."

The two brothers did not travel the same religious path for very long. Francis went along with John to Oxford in 1821, where John continued to coach him for entrance into the University. The two brothers were often in conflict, however, and John's journals show repeated self-reproaches and deprecations. He was especially troubled at his own bad temper, frequent anger and "cruelty" towards Francis. Years later he wrote and asked his brother's forgiveness for the way he had treated him during those years.

On his part, Francis would later become a follower of J. N. Darby's Plymouth Brethren, even serving as a fledgling and totally unsuccessful missionary in the Moslem Near East for a short time. His religious path diverged sharply from John's and Francis eventually became a prominent Unitarian.

In 1822, John was ready to take the examination for admission as a Fellow of Oriel College. It was a harrowing experience, especially in light of his failure at Trinity, but prayerfully and soberly he went through it. He prayed, "Thou seest how fondly, and I fear idolatrously, my affections are set on succeeding at Oriel. Take away all hope, stop not an instant, O my God, if doing so will gain me Thy Spirit." But this time the outcome was different, and on Friday, April 12, 1822, he was greeted in the Common Room of Oriel by his new colleagues, and later wrote in his journal, "Thank God, thank God."

At Oriel, John soon became closely associated with Richard Whately, later Archbishop of Dublin. Writing of Whately in his *Apologia* in 1859, Newman says, "Mr. Whately...showed great kindness to me. He renewed it in 1825, when he became Principal of Alban Hall, making me his Vice-Principal and Tutor.... I owe a great deal to him. He was a man of generous and warm heart... While I was still awkward and timid in 1822, he took me by the hand and acted toward me the part of a gentle and encouraging instructor. He emphatically opened my mind and taught me to think and to use my reason. After being first noticed by him in 1822, I became very intimate with him in 1825, when I was Vice-Principal at Alban Hall. I gave up that office in 1826 when I became Tutor of my College, and his hold on me gradually relaxed. He had done his work towards me, or nearly so, when he taught me to see with my own eyes and walk with my own feet. Not that I had not a good deal to learn from others still, but I influenced them as well as they me, and co-operated rather than merely concurred with them."[3]

This period has been termed Newman's "incipient liberal" period. He admits to having ignorantly criticized "some of the verses" in the Athanasian Creed as being unnecessarily scientific. He used "flippant language" against the Fathers, "about whom I knew little at the time," and he questioned some of the miracles of the early Church. "The truth is," he confesses, "I was beginning to prefer intellectual excellence to moral; I was drifting in the direction of the Liberalism of the day." This drift was brought to an abrupt halt "by two great blows: illness and bereavement."

Illness came in the form of a kind of nervous collapse which was due to emotional strain and overwork. In the fall of 1827, the Newman family finances were in great hardship, and John was left with the responsibility of largely filling the need. In addition, affairs at Oriel were such that he was greatly concerned about the improvement he was seeking to bring about there. A new Provost had been chosen and Newman played a key role in that choice. Suddenly, he found himself in "confusion, an inability to think or recollect." It was diagnosed as "over exertion of the brain, with a disordered stomach." Bleeding with leeches and a period of rest were prescribed.

Bereavement came with the death of his 19-year old sister, Mary, in January, 1828. She was suddenly stricken during dinner, and died a few hours later. It was a severe blow to the whole family, and an even greater one to John who thought that he "loved her too well." That spring, as he rode through the countryside, he thought of Mary's death and his own strange encounter with the slim thread by which we hold consciousness and even life itself. He saw the intellectual path on which he had been drifting to be what it was — mortal, ephemeral, capable of being wiped out in the blink of an eye. It was in the same year that Newman became Vicar of St. Mary's Church, Oxford.

These two events coincided with John's increasing friendship with young Hurrell Froude, and the marriage of two of his best friends, Edward B. Pusey and John Bowden. Froude was the son of an Archdeacon, brought up in the old "High Church and High Tory" tradition of the Church of England. This group within the Church of England had not been friendly to the Puritan, Wesleyan and Evangelical influence in the Church. Froude, although younger than Newman, exercised a very great influence on him during this period. Since John had already left the rather narrow confines of his earlier Evangelicalism under the tutelage of Richard Whately and the intellectuals at Oxford, with the collapse of his faith in the Liberal approach, he needed something more substantial on which to lean. Already his reading of the ancient Church Fathers and the High Church thinkers of the previous centuries had prepared him to hear what Froude thought and believed. "His opinions arrested me," he writes, "even when they did not gain my assent." Froude openly professed his admiration for the Church of Rome, and his hatred of the Reformers. He delighted in the notion of an hierarchical system, of sacerdotal power, and of full ecclesiastical liberty [meaning, from state control — *Ed.*]. He felt scorn for the maxim 'The Bible and the Bible only is the religion of Protestants,' and he gloried in accepting Tradition as a main instrument of religious teaching. He had a severe idea of the intrinsic excellence of Virginity, and he considered the Blessed Virgin Mary its great Pattern. He delighted in thinking of the Saints, he had a vivid appreciation of the idea of sanctity, its possibility and its heights; and he was more inclined to believe a large amount of miraculous interference as occuring in the early and middle ages. He embraced the principle of penance and mortification. He had a deep devotion to the Real Presence, in which he had a firm faith. . . . He took an eager and courageous view of things as a whole. I should say that his power of entering into the minds of others did not equal his other gifts; he did not believe, for instance, that I really held the Roman Church to be Anti-Christian. On many points he would not believe but that I agreed with him, when I did not. . . ."[4] Newman goes on to enumerate the additions to his theological creed which he owed to Froude, namely, admiration for the Church of Rome, dislike of the Reformation, devotion to the Blessed Virgin, and belief in the Real Presence.

In December, 1832, Newman was invited to join Froude and his father the Archdeacon, on a Mediterranean voyage, in hope that the warmer winter climate would improve young Froude's lingering lung disease [probably tuberculosis]. Concerned still about Newman's overwork with his parish and tutorial duties, and his still-frail health, Froude wrote, "It would set you up." And so they went — visiting Gibraltar, Malta, Corfu, Naples, Sicily and Rome.

"What can I say of Rome," Newman wrote, "but that it is the first of cities, and that all I ever saw are but dust (even dear Oxford inclusive) compared with this majesty and glory?" Going to St. Peter's, he wrote, "Everything is bright and clean, and Sunday is kept decorously." But as to Roman Catholicism, he still thought of it as the Antichrist. "As to the *Roman* Catholic system," he wrote to his mother, "I have ever detested it so much that I cannot detest it more by seeing it; but to the *Catholic* system I am more attached than ever, and quite love the little monks of Rome; they look so innocent and bright, poor boys!" Yet he felt that underneath the blatant and serious defects, there was a "deep substratum" of true Christianity in that Church.

News reached the travelers of a Whig-sponsored bill in the House of Commons to reorganize the Church of Ireland, eliminating 10 bishoprics. To Newman and his friends, this was treating the Church like nothing more than a governmental department. They were outraged. This would prove to be a crucial point in Newman's life, for it was one of the outward causes which would soon catapult him into the yet-to-be-formed Oxford Movement.

Newman decided to return to Sicily alone after the Froudes left for England. He had been fascinated by the ruggedness and mystery of the island, and insisted on going back in spite of the urging of his friends. In Sicily, he fell seriously ill, and was near death for ten days, with raging fever and delirium. His servant thought he was dying, and begged for his last instructions. "I gave them as he wished," he writes, "but I said, 'I shall not die.' I repeated, 'I shall not die, for I have not sinned against light, I have not sinned against light.' I have never been quite able to make out what I meant."[5] But later he was convicted that he had acted in great self-will in several areas, including the decision to travel to Sicily alone. Yet in the sickness he was sustained by "a most consoling thought of God's electing love" and his assurance that he belonged to Him.

This was the third turning point associated with illness, and he hastened back to England as soon as he was well enough to travel, believing that God had some work for him to do. It was on June 13, 1833, while on board a sailing vessel bound for home, becalmed off the coast of Sardinia, that he wrote his best-loved hymn, "Lead, Kindly Light." The hymn reflects the fruit of the soul-struggle he had undergone, and the conviction of sin which he had experienced in Sicily. "I loved to choose and see my path. . . . Remember not past years!"

The Sunday after his return to England, John Keble preached the annual Assize Sermon in St. Mary's Church in Oxford. He called the sermon "National Apostasy," and expressed the fear that duty to the Church and duty to the State might become irreconcilable. "I have ever considered and kept the day as the start of the religious movement of 1833," Newman writes.

It is one of the paradoxes of Christian history that Newman became the foremost leader of the new reform movement in the Church of England — a movement he would later abandon to enter the Roman Catholic Church. For what he and his colleagues began in "the religious movement of 1833" was nothing short of a new reformation in the Church of England — a movement which profoundly changed that Church and even affected the other Protestant Churches. It was an effort to reclaim the Catholic heritage of the pre-Reformation Church in England — relying heavily on certain High Church writers of the 18th century and a sometimes strained interpretation of the Prayer Book and the Thirty-Nine Articles.

In looking at Newman's life, it seems clear that once having embraced the Anglo-Catholic position, moving away emotionally and intellectually from his Evangelical beginnings, he and the others were zealous for their cause — zealous to the point of incurring fear, suspicion and hostility within the very Church they had set out to save. "I had supreme confidence in our cause," he writes. "We were upholding primitive Christianity which was delivered for all time by the early teachers of the Church, and which was registered and attested to in the Anglican formularies and by the Anglican divines. That ancient religion had well nigh faded away out of the land, through the political changes of the last 150 years, and it must be restored. It would be in fact a second Reformation — a better reformation, for it would not be a return to the 16th century, but to the 17th."[6]

The enemy, as they perceived it, was Erastianism — the subservience of the Church to the State. This policy had caused no great difficulty as long as the State was in Tory hands, but now the Whigs were in the driver's seat, and no time was to be lost. Something of the spirit with which this battle was undertaken is seen in Newman's admission that he "despised every rival system of doctrine and its arguments too. . . . I dare say [my bearing] gave offense to many. . . ."[7]

One of those who was offended by Newman's "bearing" was Thomas Arnold, Headmaster of Rugby. Arnold's Christianity was of the Liberal type, emphasizing its influence on character and good works. He felt

Newman had joined the forces of reaction, and he was insulted when it was reported that Newman had, in a casual conversation in Rome, implied criticism of him with the question, "But is Arnold a Christian?" Arnold wrote indignantly that the insult "had all the ill effects of falsehood, not without some portion of its guilt." Newman replied that in his view, Dr. Arnold's ecclesiastical principles were "unscriptural, unchristian and open to ecclesiastical censure."

In many quarters Newman was earning the reputation for bigotry and arrogance. When we look at this characteristic of his from a spiritual standpoint, it is easier to understand why God allowed the repeated buffetings of misunderstanding and even of injustice to beat against him. And it is the mark of his spiritual greatness and the unswerving commitment to his original commitment to the Lord that such experiences did not embitter him, but made him more tolerant and sympathetic toward those who disagreed with him. The contrast between the Newman who leapt into the Tractarian movement in 1833 and the Newman who was raised to the Cardinalate in 1879 show how adversity and misunderstandings, mistakes and failures had all worked to fashion the spirit of the man toward sainthood.

His involvement in the Tractarian movement (another name for the Oxford Movement) caused problems at Oxford, and a breach with his former mentor and friend, Richard Whately. But as vicar of St. Mary's, the University Church, Newman drew a steadily growing following of young men who were convinced by his logic and attracted by his evident sincerity and godly life. One of those who often came to hear him wrote later, "After hearing those sermons, you might come away still not believing the tenets peculiar to the High Church system; but you would be harder than most men if you did not feel more than ever ashamed of coarseness, selfishness, worldliness, if you did not feel the things of faith brought closer to the soul. His appeal was primarily to the heart and not to the mind."[8]

The small group of dedicated Tractarians had set themselves to stir up the Church with a call to its Catholic heritage. This they felt they could do best by writing "Tracts for the Times" on various subjects. In all, a total of ninety tracts were produced between 1833 and 1843. Fighting the charge of preaching "Popery," Newman published a series of lectures in 1837 entitled *The Prophetical Office of the Church, Viewed Relatively to Romanism and Popular Protestantism*, in which he proclaimed Anglicanism as the *Via Media* — a term still in use, but which he would later repudiate. He saw the Anglican Church, as it was being reformed by the Tractarians, as holding a middle ground in keeping with the undivided Church of previous centuries. Rome, he believed, had added superstitions to the original body of truth, while Protestants had "capriciously subtracted" from it. Protestantism, he felt, inevitably tended towards Liberalism and Unitarianism.

It was an important element in his belief that the Church was, in a sense, infallible. It was impossible, he argued later, that God would not guard and preserve the truth He had entrusted to the Church — and it was the authority of the Church to define what the true interpretation of the faith should be when grave questions arose in the minds of the faithful. With a manful attempt to interpret the Thirty Nine Articles in such a way that they would present no undue problem to the catholic mind, he issued Tract 90 in 1841. The effect was immediate and thunderous. Classrooms and pulpits denounced the work, and Newman was called a traitor to the Church of England, an "evasive hypocrite" pretending to be an Anglican but cloaking a secret Romanist heart.

Under advice from the Archbishop of Canterbury, the Bishop of Oxford requested Newman to withdraw Tract 90 and to discontinue publication of the tracts altogether. Newman hesitated, since he had received no official censure. A compromise was then worked out, in which Tract 90 would not be censured, but the tracts would be stopped. Newman was also required to send the bishop a public letter repudiating the claims of Rome and stating his believe that the Anglican Church was "the Catholic Church in this country." This seemed to allay the storm for the moment.

Attached to the parish of St. Mary's was a kind of mission church at Littlemore, a few miles away. There Newman had built a church a few years before, and for a time he had toyed with the idea of beginning a small monastic house there. The first Anglican sister had made her vows to Newman and Edward B. Pusey in 1841. She would become the first Superior of the Convent of the Holy and Undivided Trinity at Oxford eight years later. In 1842, however, knowing that establishing a monastic house at Littlemore was out of the question, Newman decided to take a row of stables on some property he owned and convert them into cell-like rooms. Into these he moved that year to escape the continuing storm over Tract 90, to develop his own life of prayer, to devote himself to the care of the Littlemore flock and to work on a translation of St. Athanasius. It was a time of great pain and inner conflict for him. His own convictions about what the Church of England *should be* ran counter to what it in fact *was*. Rome, on the other hand, seemed full of superstition.

Other developments added to his uncertainty and difficulty. Plans were being made by the government, in collaboration with the bishops, to establish a joint

Anglican-Lutheran bishopric in Jerusalem — in the view of the Tractarians an unacceptable compromise with heresy!

At Littlemore, in the midst of rumors and accusations that an "Anglo-Catholic monastery" was being erected there, Newman moved into his converted stables, soon to be joined by several young men who were leaning strongly towards Roman Catholicism. One of them, Ambrose St. John, would remain with him for the rest of his life, Newman's closest and dearest friend and aide. Having been told by his bishop not to write about the Tracts or the Thirty Nine Articles, Newman began seriously to consider resigning from St. Mary's. His own doubts about the Church of England made him increasingly uncomfortable in it. Frustrated on every side, yet still uncertain about Rome, he decided there was only one honorable course — resignation. At first he hoped to serve the Littlemore Church, but that proved to be impossible. So on September 24, 1843, he preached his last sermon at St. Mary's, which he entitled "The Parting of Friends," ending with a request that his brethren would "remember him in time to come though you hear him not, and pray for him, that in all things he may know God's will, and at all times be ready to fulfill it."

By 1844, some twenty-four bishops had publicly condemned Tract 90. At first Newman intended to protest, but then he "gave up the thought in despair." Against his earlier promise, Bishop Bagot of Oxford joined his mild condemnation of the Tract to that of the other bishops. Writing to another famous convert, Edward Manning (later Archbishop and Cardinal) about his resignation from St. Mary's, Newman says, "This has been caused by the general repudiation of the view, contained in No. 90, on the part of the Church. I could

not stand against such an unanimous expression of opinion from the Bishops, supported as it has been, by the
acquiescence, or at least silence, of all classes in the
Church, lay and clerical. If there ever was a case in
which an individual teacher has been put aside and vir-
tually put away by a community, mine is one. No
decency has been observed in the attacks on me from
authority, no protests have been offered against them.
It is felt — I am far from denying, justly felt — that I
am foreign material, and cannot assimilate with the
Church of England."

It would take some additional time, a great deal of
questioning and soul-searching, before Newman would
leave the Church of his baptism and be received into
the Roman Catholic Church. Writing later about his
mental difficulties, he said that the writings of St.
Alphonsus "as I knew them by the extracts commonly
made from them, prejudiced me as much against the
Roman Church as anything else, on account of what
was called their 'Mariolatry'. . . ." The devotional "excesses" as he saw them, "had been my great *crux* as
regards Catholicism."[9]

In struggling through these difficulties, he wrote
what has become one of his most important and influential books. The book, *An Essay on Development*,
satisfied him that the additions to ancient dogmas and
practices which had been introduced in the Church of
Rome were in fact legitimate and logical outgrowths of
what was believed or implied in earlier centuries. He
wrote, ". . . from the nature of the human mind, time is
necessary for the full comprehension and perfection of
great ideas." Although these ideas have been revealed
once for all, they "could not be comprehended all at
once by the recipients, but as being received and trans-

mitted by minds not inspired and through media which were human, have required only the longer time and deeper thought for their full elucidation."[10]

These developments included the canon of the New Testament, the doctrines of original sin and infant baptism, the divine nature of Christ, communion for the laity in one kind, the infallibility of the Church over private interpretation of Scripture, the veneration of the Blessed Virgin Mary, the cult of the saints, and the supremacy of the Papacy. Some of these things had given Newman a great deal of trouble personally, and the book was really his way of satisfying himself as to the legitimacy of the Roman position. Writing later as a mature Catholic, he admits that he is still not comfortable with some of the devotional practices in regard to the Blessed Virgin. "I do not fully enter into them now; I trust I do not love her less because I cannot enter into them." He goes on to explain that "from a boy I had been led to consider that my Maker and I, His creature, were the two beings, luminously such, *in rerum natura*." Convinced that the excesses result from popular piety rather than of official Catholic teaching, he adds, "I know full well now, and did not know then, that the Catholic Church allows no image of any sort, material or immaterial, no dogmatic symbol, no rite, no sacramental, no Saint, not even the Blessed Virgin herself, to come between the soul and its Creator. It is face to face, *solus cum solo*, in all matters between man and his God. He alone creates; He alone has redeemed; before His awful eyes we go in death; in the vision of Him is our eternal beatitude."[11]

Two years after he resigned from St. Mary's, on October 8, 1845, Newman and two companions were admitted into the Roman Catholic Church, by Father

Dominic Barberi, an Italian Passionist missionary priest, in the private chapel at Littlemore. Several of his young companions had already preceded him in the decision.

Newman was almost forty-five years old. He had a rich and widely-known ministry behind him. Ahead lay another forty-five years as a Roman Catholic. In recent years, in the ecumenical atmosphere of Vatican II, the inner unity of these two halves of Newman's life had become better understood and appreciated. Far from becoming something new, Newman took into his Catholic life much of what had been there from the beginning — especially his life of prayer and his personal relationship with God. Theological and political considerations undoubtedly played an important role in his transfer from Anglican to Roman Catholicism, but studies have amply shown that Newman the Anglican and Newman the Oratorian were one and the same man. The spirituality of his life as a Catholic was indeed a flowering and development of the spiritual principles by which he had lived earlier — not a denial of them.

Newman and Ambrose St. John went to Rome in the fall of 1846, where they were prepared for and received re-ordination as priests. Here also, Newman decided on the Oratorian form of life for himself and the small band of followers back in England who were already living in a semi-monastic fashion at Olcott under the supervision of Bishop Wiseman of Birmingham. Believing the Oratorian life best suited for the purpose of furthering the Catholic faith in England, especially among the better educated classes, Newman and St. John secured papal approval of their project, with Newman being appointed Superior of a house to be established in Birmingham.

But if Newman expected to be free from misunderstanding — and even persecution — now that he had gone over to Rome, disappointment awaited him. From within the Church and even from the Oratorian life itself, he was to experience many a heartache and care. Back in England, a small group of enthusiastic converts under the leadership of Fr. Frederick William Faber, were eager to become Oratorians. But they never seemed to grasp nor fully accept Newman's understanding of the Oratorian life and spirituality. As a result, a second Oratory was established in London, with Faber appointed by Newman as Superior. The two houses soon began to diverge in their approach to Catholic life and ministry, and relations between them became increasingly strained. For some years an almost complete breach existed between them, which caused Newman hurt and grief.

Another incident in this period was the cause of much anguish. With the restoration of the Roman hierarchy in England in 1850, a new wave of anti-papal feeling rose. The Protestant Alliance was formed to counter the Roman influence, and under its sponsorship, an ex-Dominican priest, Giacinto Achilli, came to London, where he published a book, *Dealing with the Inquisition.* Cardinal Wiseman, newly named archbishop of Westminster, wrote an article exposing Achilli's moral irregularities, and Newman in Birmingham made specific criticisms of Achilli. Again, supported by the Protestant Alliance, Achilli brought a suit of criminal libel against Newman, and won a judgment against him in 1852. Although the expenses were borne by loyal supporters in England, Europe and America, the entire Achilli affair weighed heavily on Newman.

In 1851, Newman was asked to establish a Catholic University in Dublin — a project he undertook with the understanding that he could maintain his intimate relationship with the Birmingham Oratory. He published a series of lectures on what he felt a Catholic university should be, entitled *The Idea of a University.* It called for an integration and unity of all branches of human learning, against the fragmentation and specialization that increasingly marked modern education. His ideas are still relevant, especially to Christian education, and his work is considered basic in the field.

Lack of cooperation from the Irish bishops, differences of opinions as to the desirability of a new university, and a lingering suspicion of Newman in the minds of some of the more zealous converts from Anglicanism, all combined to frustrate the Catholic University plan. After four years, Newman resigned and returned to his Oratory. The university languished for the next twenty years, until it was re-established under new auspices. Again, the frustration of misunderstanding and failure dogged his steps.

In 1857, he was asked by the Catholic bishops to make a new English translation of the Bible. But after several years of frustration, even expending his own funds on the project, he was forced to abandon it. During this time his relations with Fr. Faber were more and more strained. Faber had become identified with the ultramontane party in the Church — a group which held to the most extreme interpretation of the Pope's authority and infallibility. In 1858, Newman was asked by the English hierarchy to become editor of a Catholic periodical, *The Rambler.* A short time later he wrote an article entitled *On Consulting the Faithful in Matters of Doctrine,* in which he pointed out that in earlier centuries "the faithful" remained orthodox while the bishops had been tolerant of the heresy of Arianism. The true Faith, he said, was saved in the 4th century, "not by the unswerving firmness of the Holy See, Councils or bishops, but by the *consensus fidelium.*" It was one of his bedrock convictions that what was believed at all times by the whole Church was normative Christian doctrine — an idea he had learned much earlier from St. Augustine. His essay was termed by Bishop Brown of Newport, one "which might have been the writing of a Calvinist." So great was the storm it evoked that Cardinal Wiseman required him to submit a detailed explanation of his views to demonstrate his loyalty to the Holy See. The explanation was shown to authorities in England, but it was never relayed to the Pope or any authority in Rome. At this point, Newman feared to go to Rome to try to defend himself, his loyalty to the Pope continued to be suspect, and his name was not cleared until 1867.

There were forces and persons in high places in the Catholic Church who were not friendly to Newman. Some of these had the ear of the reigning pontiff, Pius IX, who was fighting a losing battle to keep possession of the Papal States against the forces fighting for a unified Italy. When the *Rambler* questioned the desirability of having the papacy involved as a temporal power, it was considered disloyal by many. Newman resigned from his association with the *Rambler*, but he remained under a cloud of suspicion. A period of self-imposed silence followed, a time when Newman's life reached what has been called its "low-water mark." As his despondency and discouragement came to be generally known, rumors began to circulate that he was contemplating returning to the Anglican Church, rumors he was finally forced to answer with a strong denial published in the London *Globe*. There was even a report that he was seen in Littlemore, leaning over a gatepost weeping. The Cross was certainly being applied heavily to whatever was left of ambition or hope of doing some great work. Not only was he cut off from his old friends and associates of Oxford days, but he was blocked by invisible enemies, working behind the scenes, in the Church he had chosen and had come to love.

In 1864 another attack came from a different quarter which roused Newman to action and was instrumental in breaking his self-imposed silence. An Anglican clergyman, Rev. Charles Kingsley, a well-known and popular author, wrote a review of a book of Anthony Froude (brother of Newman's old friend, Hurrell Froude) in *MacMillan's Magazine.* In his review Kingsley took the opportunity to call Newman's truthfulness into question. He quoted Newman as saying, "Truth for its own sake has never been a virtue with the Roman clergy. Fr. Newman informs us that it need not be, and on the whole ought not to be; that cunning is the weapon which Heaven has given to the Saints wherewith to withstand the brute male force of the wicked world...." Newman demanded to know where Kingsley had ever found such a statement by him. Kingsley replied that he referred to *Sermons on the Subject of the Day, No. xx,* in a volume published in 1844, entitled, "Wisdom and Innocence." Newman answered that the sermon referred to was preached while he was still an Anglican, and that he had never uttered the words being attributed to him. Kingsley then published an "apology" which, instead of admitting his wrongness, intimated that nothing Newman said could really be trusted. "What, then, does Dr. Newman mean?" he asked.

Since the controversy had begun publicly, there was no question of a private conclusion. So, to set the record straight, Newman decided it was time to present to the public — Catholic and Protestant — a clear record of his "religious opinions" as they had developed and changed over the years. The record — released in the form of successive pamphlets — was his most famous work, *Apologia pro Vita Sua.* It is still regarded by many as the greatest spiritual autobiography ever written in English.

The book catapulted him again into the limelight, convincing his fellow Catholics of his sincerity and Protestants of the possibility "of accepting Roman Catholicism on the basis of freely exercised logic."[12]

The book completely vindicated his character in the eyes of the world. During its writing, however, he was under a presentiment of impending death. In that frame of heart he wrote his only long, dramatic poem, *The Dream of Gerontius,* picturing a dying man facing the judgment of God. *Gerontius* was an immediate success, and was republished several times. Sir Edward Elgar would set it to music in 1900. Some of its verses still appear in hymnals as "Praise to the Holiest in the Heights."

After his departure from Littlemore in 1845, he was not to return to Oxford for thirty-one years. Concerned about the lack of a Catholic ministry to the Catholic students at the university, it had long been his hope to see an Oratory or hall set up in Oxford. At first he was rebuffed by the English bishops, who still feared the influence of Oxford and strongly discouraged Catholics from attending it or any Protestant university. In 1866, Bishop Ullathorne suggested that Newman's project be reconsidered, and the matter was referred to Rome. After some ecclesiastical maneuvering, Ullathorne was able to inform Newman that Rome had granted permission for an Oratory in Oxford, with Newman as the inaugurator of the project. Four months later, however, a letter from the bishop prohibited him from going to Oxford himself. Again, his adversaries had succeeded in blocking his plans. Promising "hearty obedience,"

Newman was nonetheless deeply hurt by this new blow. It is one of the paradoxes of his life that today Newman's name is honored in student clubs or centers in colleges and universities throughout the world.

Pius IX had issued the dogma of the Immaculate Conception in 1854, and Newman had given hearty support to its promulgation. But when, under the pressure of the loss of the Papal States and the temporal power of the papacy, there was agitation for a General Council to declare the infallibility of the Pope, Newman was "less than enthusiastic." He saw no crisis of faith which would justify a General Council. Knowing that some of the extreme papal party, the Ultramontanes, were agitating for a definition of infallibility that would encompass almost anything that came from the Pope's hand, Newman feared the results would be especially harmful to the Church's interest in England, which still held an irrational fear of papal power. To make matters even more difficult for him, the London Oratory and his fellow convert, Edward (now Cardinal) Manning were lined up on the side of the Ultramontanes. They considered that the declaration of infallibility would be a kind of insurance against further erosion of the Pope's power in the face of his loss of his last temporal rule. To avoid becoming embroiled in the controversy, Newman declined a personal invitation from Pius IX to attend the first Vatican Council.

A private letter which Newman wrote to Bishop Ullathorne, expressing his grave misgivings about the wisdom of proclaiming a dogma of infallibility, Newman said, "When we are at rest and have no doubts — and at least practically... hold the Holy Father to be infallible, suddenly there is thunder in the clear sky, and we are told to prepare for something, we know not what, to try our faith, we know not how.... What have we done to be treated as the faithful were never treated before?... Why should an aggressive and insolent faction be allowed to 'make the heart of the just sad, whom the Lord has not made sorrowful'?"[13]

The letter became public, and the battle was joined. Newman was ranked on the side of those who opposed the decree. When the decree on Infallibility was issued following the hasty end to the Vatican Council, a minority of those who had opposed it withdrew from Roman obedience and became the "Old Catholics," a body still existing today. Others who had opposed the decree acquiesced, willingly or hesitantly. But the statement was very much more limited in scope than the Ultramontanes had wished. Newman himself had no difficulty with its careful language, and always expressed willingness to have his own views brought under authority. He did have a great deal of trouble, however, with Cardinal Manning's "extravagant" interpretation. Such was the cloud remaining over his name in Rome, however, that he did not feel it wise to write further on the subject. "If I did speak, I should be reported to Rome," he said, "perhaps put on the Index [of forbidden books or writers], perhaps reproved, and thus should make matters worse instead of better."

The Vatican Council ended in 1870 shortly after the Italian troops occupied Rome. Anti-clerical campaigns continued for a time in France, Spain and Italy, and serious opposition to the Dogma of Papal Infallibility was raised in Germany and Austria. In England, Archbishop Manning published a lecture entitled "Caesarism and Ultramontanism," picturing the ongoing struggle between papal power and civil power. The effect could have been predicted. Pius IX had issued his *Syllabus of Errors* in 1864, condemning, among other things (80 items in all) the idea that national churches could be

separated from the authority of the Pope, that Protestantism is another form of the Christian religion in
which it is as possible to be pleasing to God as in the
Roman Catholic Church; that kings and princes are not
under the jurisdiction of the Church; and that it was no
longer expedient that the Catholic religion should be
the only religion of the state to the exclusion of other
forms of worship.[14] The *Syllabus* had already caused a
stir of concern, and now that the idea of infallibility
was being stretched to the limit, it was little wonder
that it raised a new outcry. William E. Gladstone, a
staunch Evangelical and leader of the Liberals in Parliament (later Prime Minister), published a protest
called *The Vatican Decrees and Their Bearing on Civil
Allegiance*, raising the spectre that Roman Catholicism
and loyalty to civil authority were now incompatible.[15]

Knowing that many Catholics themselves were
uneasy with Manning's intrepretation of infallibility,
and feeling the need to ease their minds as well as the
mind of the English public, Newman decided to write *A
Letter to His Grace the Duke of Norfolk on the Occasion of Mr. Gladstone's Recent Expostulation*. It was
published in January, 1875. In it he set forth clearly the
careful limitations on papal infallibility which had been
hammered out in the Vatican Council. Infallibility of
the Pope applies only on matters of faith and morals
when he speaks *ex cathedra* as the Universal Teacher of
the Catholic Church. It must be clearly announced and
understood to be such a declaration, because infallibility
does not extend to the Pope's personal life and thoughts,
nor to his decisions as ruler either of a temporal state or
of the Church.

Speaking of the role of conscience, Newman says
that infallibility has to do with abstracts, while the conscience relates to action. Freedom of conscience, how-

ever, is not license to selfishness, "the right of thinking, speaking, writing or acting according to one's judgment. . ., without any thought of God at all." He concludes that it would be an unusual thing for a Pope's general condemnation or proposition to conflict with one's conscience. The work won the admiration even of Cardinal Manning, who staunchly defended it when it was attacked in Rome. Pius IX was reported to have found "some objectionable passages" in it, but added that he understood that good had been accomplished by it and that he had no further doubts about Newman's loyalty to the Holy See. His remarks, however, were never relayed to Newman himself.

The *Letter* brought Newman a renewed wave of recognition and appreciation from Catholics and Protestants in England. Even Gladstone acknowledged the grace and skill of his answer. But it was Newman's lifelong belief that good fortune must be balanced by bad. Bad fortune came this time with the death of his dearest friend, Ambrose St. John, a blow from which Newman at seventy never fully recovered. He wrote to a friend, "I feel that this was needed. . . . This alone can wean me from [this world]; to see those dear to me, one after another depart, as they have been departing during these last five years."[16]

But there was more good fortune in store. In December, 1877, word came from his old Oxford school, Trinity College, that they wanted to make him their first Honorary Fellow. Remembering the Oxford difficulties of the past, Newman was careful first to obtain permission of his brother Oratorians and of Bishop Ullathorne before accepting the honor. But it was a great and joyful day when for the first time in thirty-two years he returned to the scenes he had loved so well. While he was at Oxford, he visited Littlemore, too, and visited his mother's garden there. There was a joyful and tender reunion between him and his old friend of Tractarian days, Edward B. Pusey, who was still the grand old man of Catholic-minded Anglicans. One can see the fruit of a life of devotion and spiritual growth. Instead of having become bitter in the midst of the many controversies that raged about him, he had shown greatness of heart and resilience of spirit. The cross had been applied to the arrogant and "righteous overmuch" spirit of which he wrote when he was young. Without compromising his convictions, he could move with more freedom among those who disagreed with him. And through the working of the pain of rejection and misunderstanding, his writings would carry a breadth of spirit which would become more widely appreciated in generations to come.

Pius IX died the next year, old and full of years. His had been the longest pontificate in history, and the latter part, especially, had been spent in a desperate and sometimes futile fight against the tide of modernism. His successor, Leo XIII, came to the Chair of Peter with the intention to restore a sense of balance to the Church.

That summer a representative of the most influential Catholic laymen in England went to Cardinal Manning with a request that Newman be made a Cardinal. In later years, Pope Leo is reported as saying to a friend of Newman, "My cardinal! It was not easy! They said he was too liberal; but I had determined to honor the Church in honoring Newman...."[17] And so the offer of the cardinal's hat was extended. Making sure he would be allowed to remain in the Oratory in Birmingham (most Cardinals were expected to live in Rome unless they were functioning bishops), Newman gratefully accepted. Records indicate that Manning was a reluctant participant in the honor, if not in downright opposition to it. After much delay and some strange confusions in communications, Newman went to Rome and received the red hat in May, 1879. He chose as the motto of his cardinalate the words, *Cor ad cor loquitur* — heart speaks to heart.

His homecoming was something of a triumphal entry. Greeted by his brother Oratorians and the Catholic dignitaries of the city, he entered the Church, knelt and prayed at the high altar, and then took the seat that had been placed in the center of the sanctuary for him. His words were slow, with frequent pauses — caused, no doubt, by the emotion of the occasion. He began, "It is such happiness to come *home*." He was now in his seventy-ninth year.

The last eleven years of his life were aptly characterized by one of his remarks: "The cloud is lifted from me forever." His activities continued to diminish, but he was ever alert to the needs of his Oratory and of the Catholic cause in England. One of his last articles expressed his grave fear that human reason unbridled can lead us astray, and upheld again the needed role of the Catholic Church as the custodian of divine truth.

Of his life and work, the *Oxford Dictionary* says, "Though unsuccessful in most of his undertakings in the Roman Catholic Church during his lifetime, his genius has come to be more and more recognized after his death, and his influence both on the restoration of Roman Catholicism in England and the advance of Catholic ideas in the Church of England can hardly be exaggerated."[18]

A well-known Newman scholar says, "It might seem that [his] conversion brought him into the Church on the eve of the Church's own disintegration. Let us rather say that he was called, without realizing it himself, to awaken within the Catholic Church of today what she needs in order to reveal herself again to the world as the one true Church which that world so badly needs, now as ever."[19]

When he died in 1890, at the age of 89, he had lived to see his reputation restored, both in the Church and in the English mind. He had refused to allow the mis-understandings, his own mistakes and misjudgments, and the malice of those who opposed him to make him bitter. Instead, he wore his honors with humility and humor, and continued to pray to be faithful to the light he was given. He knew that he could expect that there would be light enough for the next step, and that was enough. Of him one modern admirer has written, "He was as sincere as light."[20]

Another says, "Now that the children of the Refor-mation are rediscovering community and the children of the Church freedom and responsibility, what better guide can we hope for than the man who learned the best out of both traditions — who sacrificed so much to come into the one fold, but would never give up the personal freedom which he had found outside it, which he knew should exist within it, but which at that time was not evident there."[21]

When he was buried by the side of Ambrose St. John in the cemetery which he himself had bought and given to the Birmingham Oratory, he had inscribed on his gravestone the simple words:

Ex Umbris et Imaginibus in Veritatem
From shadows and images into the Truth.

Those words are a fitting epitaph of one who through many a year of shadows and darkness con-tinued faithfully to follow the Kindly Light as he understood it. All who seek to follow that Light can pray the prayer he bequeathed to us:

O Lord, support us all the day long of this troublous life, until the shadows lengthen and the evening comes, the busy world is hushed, and the fever of life is over, and our work is done. Then, Lord, in Thy mercy, grant us a safe lodging, a holy rest, and peace at the last; through Jesus Christ our Lord. Amen.

NOTES AND REFERENCES

[1]These quotations from Newman's journals are taken from the two-volume work by Meriol Trevor, *Newman, The Pillar and the Cloud* and *Newman, Light in Winter*. Garden City: Doubleday & Company. 1959 and 1963.

[2]Or the "saved" and the "unsaved."

[3]John Henry Newman, *Apologia pro Vita Sua*.

[4]*Ibid.*

[5]*Ibid.*

[6]*Ibid.* p. 40.

[7]*Ibid.* p. 40.

[8]Quoted in Lapati, pp. 33-34. (Lapati, Americo D., *John Henry Newman*. Twayne Publishers, Inc., New York, c. 1972)

[9]*Apologia.*

[10]Newman, *Essay on Development, pp. 28-29.*

– – *Apologia.*

[12]Lapati, p. 96.

[13]Quoted in Trevor, *Light in Winter*, p. 476.

[14]See Latourette, *History of Christianity*, pp. 1099-1101 for fuller discussion of the Syllabus of Errors.

[15][A spectre raised anew in the U. S. Presidential election of 1960.]

[16]Quoted by Trevor, *op. cit.*, p. 528.

[17]*Ibid.* p. 552.

[18]*Oxford Dictionary of the Christian Church*, p. 966. (Oxford University Press, 1978.)

[19]Fr. Louis Bouyer, *Newman's Vision of Faith*, Introduction.

[20]Muriel Spark, Foreword in *Cardinal Newman's Best Plain Sermons*, Ed. Blehl, Vincent Ferrer. Herder and Herder, NY 1964.

[21]Meriol Trevor, Introduction, *Meditations and Devotions*, p. xiii., 1964. Burns & Oates, Lt. London.

BIBLIOGRAPHY

BIOGRAPHY

Trevor, Meriol, *The Pillar of the Cloud*, 1961 and *Light in Winter*, 1963, "the most complete biography."

Mozley, Anne, *Letters and Correspondence of J. H. Newman during his life in the English Church.* 1891, 2 volumes.

Ward, Wilfred, *The Life and Times of John Henry Cardinal Newman*, 1912, (reprinted in 1970).

NEWMAN'S WRITINGS

Parochial and Plain Sermons (Preached at St. Mary's Church, Oxford during Newman's Anglican days), 6 volumes. Christian Classics.

Essay on the Development of Christian Doctrine (1845).

Discourses to Mixed Congregations (1849).

Lectures on Certain Difficulties Felt by Anglicans in Catholic Teaching (1850). Wesminster, MD., Christian Classics, 1969.

On Consulting the Faithful in Matters of Doctrine (From the *Rambler*, 1859). Ed. by John Coulson. New York: Sheed and Ward.

Apologia Pro Vita Sua. 1864, 1865. Many editions available.

Meditations and Devotions. (Published posthumously in 1893).

EDITED COLLECTIONS OF NEWMAN'S WORKS

Blehl, Vincent Ferrer (ed), *Cardinal Newman's Best Plain Sermons.* Foreword by Muriel Spark. New York: Herder and Herder, 1964.

Gornall, Thomas (ed.), *Letters and Diaries of J. H. Newman.* London: 1973.

Przywara, Erich (ed.), *The Heart of Newman: A Synthesis.* New York: Sheed and Ward, 1945. Also Springfield, IL: Templegate, 1963.

Tristam, Henry (ed.), *Living Thoughts of Cardinal Newman.* New York: McKay, 1953.

HISTORICAL AND CRITICAL

Coulson, John and A. M. Allchin (eds.), *The Rediscovery of Newman: An Oxford Symposium.* 1967.

Blehl, Vincent Ferrer and Francis X. Connolly (eds.), *Newman's Apologia: A Classic Reconsidered.* [A Symposium on the *Apologia* held at Fordham University, October, 1963.] New York: Harcourt, Brace and World, 1964.

Guitton, Jean, *The Church and the Laity from Newman to Vatican II.* Tr. by Malachy Gerard Carroll. Staten Island, NY: Alba House, 1965.

John Henry Newman: Centenary Essays. London: Burns and Oates, 1945. [Essays by various Newman scholars.]

Reynolds, E. E., *Three Cardinals* [Newman-Wiseman-Manning]. New York: P. J. Kenedy and Sons, 1958.

Ryan, Alvan S. (ed.), *Newman and Gladstone: the Vatican Decrees.* Contains W. E. Gladstone's attack on Papal Infallability and Newman's reply, "A Letter to His Grace the Duke of Norfolk."